The Ethic of Reverence for the Dead

The Moral and Psychological Connection Between the Living and the Dead

BY

TODD W. VAN BECK

DEDICATION

This book is dedicated to my wife Georgia.
Without exception she has tolerated my infirmities and I have
rejoiced in her graces.

This book was written by a funeral professional
and although careers in this profession are attached to
the Reverence for the Dead, this book is for all who value life.

CONTENTS

ACKNOWLEDGMENTS

"This is one of the slowest reads I have ever experienced. That's a compliment and here's why. It's NOT slow because it's boring or poorly written but because it seems like every sentence needs to be digested.

You consistently plant seeds and make statements that deserve or command thought. Not day dreaming but real soul searching reflection.

Here is another compliment. I even tried skipping around the pages to see if it got lighter or faster. What I found was that no matter what page I landed on, I was in the same reflective mode. I found that interesting too. You could start on any page and in moments find yourself mulling over a sentence.

I am not aware of anyone who has ever done what you're doing with this work. It's in your face dignity 101 and the why and the history. It's a profession articulation of why I get so annoyed when I hear people refer to dead people as "the body" or "a body." I try to champion a daily awareness at my office that my associates are NOT going to make a removal of a body, they are going to make a transfer of a dead person who was in life someone's loved one. There will be no embalming, dressing, casketing etc. of a body. We will embalm Mr. Smith, dress Miss Jones or casket Baby Johnson. Reverence is to the dead. It damn well does matter!

At times I wondered how a Gary O'Sullivan "pre-need sales person audience" would take to this. Maybe they would. I thought with Gino Merendino's commitment to the importance and dignity of grounds and maintenance, I bet his college class would appreciate this. And that leads me to how this also fits with the Jim Starks' cremation college as well as the Joe Marsaglia's embalming college and Mark Krause's 21st century college. What you wrote about is all about what's important and to that end, it fits everywhere in conversations or lectures about our profession. ***It's one hell of a read.***"

- **Ernie Heffner**, *Heffner Funeral Chapels & Crematory*

"Everyone involved in death, whether in funeral, cemetery or pre-need care, now possess a tool that will provoke a powerful, thoughtful and helpful blend of emotion and logic to guide them in the service and mentoring of others. True to form, Todd Van Beck shares his vision with crystal clarity and offers practical insights that cross religious, age and cultural boundaries and are sure to empower caregivers to become the professionals they wish to be. If you are concerned with the current or future status of our profession, you owe it to yourself to read this book."

- **Jeffrey Chancellor**, CFSP

INTRODUCTION

Establishing the Unavoidable Link

This book centers around one subject: the ethical care of the dead.

Central to this work is the identification, development and articulation of the absolute ethical ideal that is being called the Ethic of Reverence for the Dead.

This is not a book about grief per se, but grief must be included here and there, because the emotion of grief is so often experienced when death happens.

The contents of this book apply to every living person on earth, but not every living person on earth will find this information pleasurable.

This book addresses the ethics of taking care of dead people, and straight away this subject might startle, annoy, provoke and unsettle some readers. The author offers no apologizes if this is the reaction. No apologies are made and no candy coating of this subject is even attempted for one simple reason: the death rate is an even 100%, every living human being already is fully vested in the subject of death and their own death, regardless of how they respond to this topic.

This book is a book about dead people, pure and simple, and because of this questions are inevitably raised, such as: why all this fuss about dead people? Is there anything I can learn in thinking about dead people? I don't mind talking about death (particularly someone else's), but why talk about my own dead body?

These are indeed valid questions and as a starting point, we will explore the ideas of the Harvard thinker and psychologist William James and draw attention to the several points that he made in his seminal 1902 book by the title of *The Varieties of Religious Experience.*

In this book William James makes an extremely impressive assessment in bringing sense to the complex and powerful experiences that lay at the heart of the lives of so many people who encounter what can be called "the larger-than-life experiences."

Examples of this type of larger-than-life experience would be those who encounter a profound religious experience or those who encounter things they never have seen before, which change their lives forever, such as seeing a loved one's dead human remains for the first time. Taking this a step further this would even include simply being around the sacred dead, and then, if touched or motivated by this experience of being with the dead, to then think out the meaning of this reality and in turn, enhance one's own personal maturity.

The simple and ancient human activity of seeing, touching, spending time, and being around the dead, and most critically, how we actually treat our dead, is the basic foundation of the ethical ideal that the Ethic of Reverence for the Dead is founded upon.

Here is a beginning example of what we are referring to: I only know my friend as being alive – he has always been alive, but now he is dead, and this reality changes his life and my life permanently.

This permanent and profound change, which is clearly larger-than-life, is created because I have never seen my friend dead. He has always been alive – breathing, walking, talking, seeing, hearing, etc. Now, however, my friend is really dead and he is now permanently and profoundly much different than he was when he was alive – he cannot hear, walk, talk, see or breathe.

Let us continue our analysis of this beginning example. Because my friend is dead I am thrust into whether I like it or not, into my own "larger-than-life-experience," and I have two options open to me:

Option one is that I can choose to be with my deceased friend in his actual physical death, in the presence of his dead sacred remains; this is most times an option (if the sacred decedent is recoverable or viewable). If I select this option and allow myself to experience the reality of this experience, I can be exposed to and learn valuable life maturity lessons which are lurking silently in my choice of confronting my friend's physical death by spending time with his dead human remains. These growing up lessons could never be learned by me if my friend had not died or I chose to ignore the significance of his death.

Learn something about personal maturity from dead bodies – or worse, think about my own dead body? Have you lost your mind? On the surface this idea may easily seem absurd. What can I possibly learn from such a potentially sad and mournful experience? Regardless of my initial suspicions, lessons which will enhance my personal maturity are certainly there and possess true wisdom about continuing to live life and growing in my own self-realization.

For a start, one lesson that my confrontation with the reality of death (being in the presence of the dead) can teach me is mature insights about the harsh and unpleasant realities of life which serve as a preparatory lesson for future unpleasant realities that I will surely experience if I live long enough. It is called personal maturity or simply old-fashioned growing up. We will have more to say about "lessons" from the dead later.

I have a **second option** however. I can easily ignore the significance of my friend's death and take the option of avoiding all contact with his dead sacred remains. This is an option, but little, if any learning about maturity can ever take place by denying and avoiding life's difficult realities.

Avoidance or apathy concerning a personal participation in a basic ethical care of the dead can result in a deficiency in my own personal maturity, a slow-down in my own growing up and my own self-realization and autonomy, for I am running on inadequate and untrue information. Avoidance with the dead can and does have social and psychological consequences as we will soon learn.

Let us return to William James, as we continue our introduction. William James lists four characteristics which are common to profound life experiences: to the larger-than-life experiences and these four characteristics apply very nicely to the development of the Ethic of Reverence for the Dead.

William James 1842 – 1910

William James lists the following characteristics of what we are now calling, for simplicity's sake, the larger-than-life, and the profound and permanent life experiences such as the living encountering the dead.

First: Such experiences are "ineffable." In other words they defy expression and cannot be described adequately in mere words.

Second: Such experiences cause the people who achieve them insight into depths of truth unplumbed by the discursive intellect. In other words, no matter your IQ these experiences defy logic and ultimate understanding. Instead they come to people as illuminations, revelations which are full of significance and importance. This translates many times in people confessing that everything else that had ever happened to them was now insignificant in comparison.

Third: William James goes on to emphasize that these experiences are transient; they cannot be sustained for long. Usually they last only a few minutes, but their memory can be reproduced perfectly many years later.

Fourth: William James suggests that those who have had such an experience feel as if they have been grasped and held by a superior power.

By analyzing and building on these four characteristics taken from *The Varieties of Religious Experience*, we can identify a few more of the wisdom lessons that are potentially to be learned by seeing, touching, and actively participating in caring for the dead, but which obviously cannot be learned if the dead are ignored, brushed aside, or if their significance is underestimated to the point that their significance vanishes.

In blending the four characteristics of the larger-than-life experience which we just reviewed from *The Varieties of Religious Experience* we can now make an authentic connection when living people give attention and time to the sacred dead of the world. Here are examples of this connection:

First: People confide that when they see their dead loved one or are in the presence of the dead for the first time this experience simply defies mere words – they are speechless and confess that many times they cannot believe what they are seeing. They also are humbled in front of such a profound experience.

Second: People confide that when they see, touch and spend time with the dead they experience new insights and deeper understandings about the meaning of life which enhances their own personal maturity. For example, they ponder about how precious a gift life is, how transient and brief life is; and this type of heightened self-awareness translates into living a different type of life simply because of the fact that seeing the dead makes everything else that has ever happened to them now seems insignificant by comparison. This profound experience is particularly true in the instance of a bereaved parent who sees the sacred remains of their dead child. People also confide an awareness of a new life wisdom lesson by seeing and tending to their dead: **the urgency to live life**.

Third: Seeing a dead body for the first time usually happens in seconds, and once you have seen the dead person nothing is ever the same again. By seeing, touching and paying ethical attention to the profound significance of the dead a living person can arrive at a heightened sensitivity and awareness in that being dead is much different than being alive. Confronting the honest reality of what the actual death symbolizes quickly disenfranchises the modern fragile notion that "I would rather remember them as when they were alive."

The contemporary approach of underestimating the value of being with the dead possesses dangerous consequences for the individual who accepts such a position for in truth the dead are **NOT** alive, they are dead. This truthful realization is very important information for the affected mourners and even the larger community to have at their disposal to assist in truthful and, hence, healthy mourning and ritual activities. In addition, people who establish the reality of death in their minds also have the capacity to recall this once-in-a-lifetime experience very clearly in later years.

Fourth: People who avail themselves of this once-in-a-lifetime experience of being with and seeing to the ethical care of the dead also confide their experience of being connected with something larger and more powerful than themselves. People confide many times a type of religious experience which happens during the time they spend with the dead.

As we conclude the introduction a few remarks need to be made concerning the potential risk of this work being labeled as "old-fashioned."

As we shall see as we move through the text of this book all the reference books and all of the individual thinker's that are used in the development of this ethic are long dead, and hence the contents within this book can easily been seen as being old fashioned, as being out-of-touch, as being obsolete.

It categorically needs to be made as clear as possible to the reader that this "old-fashioned" approach was absolutely intentional by the author. No modern reference materials are used in the development of this ethical theory, and this is no accident, it is by design.

For the purposes of exploring and developing this ethical ideal concerning the ancient subject of caring for and being with the dead it is the author's contention that deep satisfaction can be found in the older ways of thinking.

However, no matter how ancient and old-fashioned the Ethic of Reverence for the Dead is it is neither antiquarian nor backwards given the fact that the human death rate is 100%. Paradoxically, this old-fashioned ethical theory speaks to our present time precisely because all people still die.

The study of the past helps us, in the present, to appreciate that these seemingly old-fashioned ideas and values were just as provisional and vital in bygone ages; it is in our present times that this ethical ideal has become shaky.

Rediscovering ethical principles and standards from texts from the past makes it clear that what we now term "the past" was once "the present," and it is our present that still proudly yet falsely regards itself that it has found the right intellectual answers or moral values that had always eluded our predecessors. Such flawed historical and ethical thinking might be popular but it is simply not true.

This then is the ethical ideal quest for a *philosophia perennis* (a perennial philosophy) which opens the door to a deeper view of reality and specifically for our purposes in the moral care of our sacred dead. This perennial philosophy underlies all things at all times – it has always been such and always will be.

I. THE GOOD STARTING POINT

The remainder of this book will examine the ethical, psycho-social and practical values of the Ethic of Reverence for the Dead. It is valuable for funeral service practitioners and lay members of all communities worldwide to periodically re-define and articulate; namely "to find again" the community values hidden in this most ignored ethical position.

It is in the essence of this ethic that not only does the ritual of the funeral find its core purpose, for without the dead there is no reason for death rituals, but also in a larger sense one discovers in the course of this ethical inquiry lessons concerning just what civilized behavior consists of in caring for the dead; and, as a result, one discovers silent insights of just what being human is about.

This ethical position is currently under an unwitting innocent conspiracy of generational silence, and hence, this subject is NOT popular.

Because of the unpopularity of any subject to do with one's own physical death (your own dead body, not someone else's) one has to look hard and courageously to identify the ethical dilemma, then discuss it, and finally prove the ethic and the accompanying moral actions that are required to put the ethic into living action.

We cannot expect to feel uplifted and carefree when this ethic is finally defined or as we continue our journey as to how this ethic affects human life for good or for bad. However, we might feel a deeper personal maturity concerning the inevitable fact of the 100% death rate statistic of which we all are included. This is the risk taken in all ethical inquiries – sometimes many times people do not feel exhilarated when the inquiry is completed.

To begin with it will be helpful to distinguish terms (there is a glossary of terms at the end of this book that the reader will want to refer to throughout the text.) The glossary expands and clarifies the narrative.

Many people pose the valid and interesting question "Is there a difference between ethics and morality?" The simple answer is yes there is.

For our purposes **ETHICS** is defined as: **a series of standards of identifying good and bad which have been carefully thought out and provided by external sources (such as a profession.) Ethics is the theory.**

For our purposes **MORALITY** is defined as: **individual actions which are taken or ignored concerning principles regarding right or wrong. Morals put the developed ethical theory into human action or not.**

There are two types of moralities, subjective and objective.

A. Subjective morality: This is the approach that morality is relative to one's own society only. Morality is determined by the individual. Morality becomes a matter of personal taste. Another term for subjective morality is "Ethical Relativism." Modern people many times subscribe to this ethical approach. This is witnessed in the common attitudes of "If it is legal and doesn't hurt anybody, go for it" or "Do your own thing".

B. Objective morality: This is the quest for an absolute objective moral.

This ethical approach asks if there are norms, principles, or standards that apply to all people everywhere. This is the approach that philosophers strive for in their work and it is not easy, certainly not as easy as subjective morality. This ethical approach carefully explores, develops and concludes the ethical position on a certain ethical topic. The Ethic of Reverence for the Dead is an example of an absolute objective moral standard and principle. It is also an ethical ideal.

What then, is **REVERENCE**? It is a mode of valuing something as sacred, rather than as a mere instrumental good to be used freely or ignored for our own purposes. To revere is to cherish in an enlightened and committed way. Reverence is more emotionally charged than the ordinary attitude of respect. Reverence is the well-developed capacity to have the feelings of awe, respect, and shame when these are the right feelings to have.

The Ethic of Reverence for the Dead is pure ethical idealism, which holds the very definition of "reverence" to be at its inviolate core. This ethic articulates the high ideal that all the dead are sacred, and are to be revered by the living as an ideal which has great worth. This ethic also holds that living people need to seriously be aware of the significance of this reverential position; it also articulates an enlightened and committed way of viewing all the dead in awe, respect, and yes even shame when the ethical care of our sacred dead is ignored.

Do I have reverential respect for them?

Hence the quest of this book is to, with great care explore, study, develop, conclude and then state an absolute ethical standard concerning what is a good and what is a bad act concerning the care of the dead worldwide. The conclusions herein will set a definition of moral guidance by developing careful and well thought out answers to the fundamental question that this ethic begs: what should we do with the dead?

II. THE BEGINNING OF THE ETHICAL JOURNEY

This is the study of how people treat each other, and what it means to lead a good life. This is pretty easy stuff, you might be thinking.

Ethics may not be what you might think it is. In the end with ethics, as strange as this might sound, nobody is **TELLING** anybody. Merely telling someone something is risky concerning just how the information was arrived at in the first place. Ethics is first and foremost **QUESTIONS**, and by asking questions, and a specific type of question in the search for truth.

The word "ethics" comes from the Greek word "ethos" meaning "character" or "custom". The ancient Greeks thought a great deal about the meaning of life and death. Because the Greeks traveled, traded, and fought wars with many different people they came to know that there were many different ways of living and believing. The Greeks began to ask questions that had never been asked before: What is mankind? What is good? What is bad? What is truth? What is love? What is beauty? What is justice?

The people who asked these and a thousand more similar questions (such as Plato and Aristotle); those who thought out and tried to supply the answers became known as teachers and philosophers. Philosophy means "the love of wisdom." The Greek philosophers held discussions and wrote out the ideas of what they meant by a good life. The ethical care of the dead, as we shall learn, is an indelible part of living a good life.

Moral behaviors were probably not very sophisticated at first; and early human beings lived much like animals. The Darwinian concept of "survival of the fittest" was the way of things. Early people had to hunt, fight and kill for food and defense. There was no protection for the individual except for their own strength and skill in fighting or in their speed and cunning in running and hiding. It was a fight or flight way of life.

However, of great interest to the purposes of this book is the fact (which will soon be explored) that even these early primitive people intentionally cared for their dead in an astonishingly specific manner.

Over time our early ancestors learned some valuable survival lessons, such as when the members and families within a tribe were at war with one another, and out of nowhere the enemy tribe made a surprise attack and stole all the food and weapons, if the tribe stayed together they could defend themselves and find safety. As a result of this the individual human being gained in person significance and importance.

The tribe also learned the growing importance and value of just one person and therefore, a hard lesson about the reality of death and the consequences of the death of one of their own. Here was the hard lesson: When someone in the tribe died it became a highly significant event first and foremost because it made the tribe weaker – the safety of everyone was put at risk. This unstable environment served as a great motivator for the tribe to respond in a ritualistic manner to their weakened condition. Rituals were the only access of coping that they immediately had at their disposal to start to bring back a community (tribal) sense of stability, unity, and affection; in other words the ritualistic behavior made them feel better, the rituals contributed to peace of mind. Interestingly, rituals still are used in our present day to accomplish this same precise task.

Consequently the death of a member of the tribe called for high level attention and action and over time this attention and action in caring for the dead was adopted and accepted by the tribe as an honored custom, it was the right thing to do.

Eventually the idea of people working and defending each other as a group became more sophisticated, and guidelines emerged as gauges to determine tribal right and wrong. These early guidelines were not as clear as our present day laws, and they were not even rules, but they were teachings and developed customs, and part of these taught customs was, as we have just seen, the reverential care of the dead. The Ethic of Reverence for the Dead emerges from these early primitive teachings and customs in tribal communities.

Over time, teachings and customs can be so habitual, people are sometimes unaware of their influence although they live and are, at times, controlled by them. This is the reason why some customary ethics are invisible. In other words we live them but aren't aware of them – they are habit. Example of this would be elections in a democratic society. The ethics behind elections is freedom and liberty. We have been voting for so long, that for many people, it becomes a habit, until the freedom and liberty is threatened. Then the philosophers bring out long-lost ethical standards and moral actions of our Founding Fathers and examine them and explore them in detail. The threat of losing our freedom and liberties creates risk, in turn possible community instability, and this renews the ethical inquiry – questions are asked, hard thinking is restored, and, just possibly, new ethical directions are decided by the voters in the next general election.

In order to identify the ethic, people need to ask questions, hard questions. To find the ethic, such as the ethic of liberty and freedom, and certainly such as the Ethic of Reverence for the Dead, one must often times look very, very hard, because sometimes ethics have been lost to the careless habitual apathy on the part of people living in history.

However, being a lost ethic does not mean the ethic is dead or does not possess valuable teaching lessons for us concerning living the good life.

Many times it is the very invisible - the lost ethic - which silently contains highly influential teachings and customs which, if resurrected, identified and put to good use, usually has very good results in our quest to live the good life. There are well thought-out reasons behind them which apply to our contemporary life even though we might well be totally unaware of their significance. The Ethic of the Reverence for the Dead qualifies as being a lost ethic.

The silent, invisible impact of lost ethics is that they still work, they are still safe and they can still give the person a sense of stability and identity which modern human beings seem to be yearning and searching to locate.

It is the purpose of this book to resurrect the Ethic of Reverence for the Dead because as we explore, in many ways this important ethic has been lost to a

great extend in the unfortunate apathetical moral attitudes that exhibit themselves in modern society.

The ethical teachings contained as, we shall see, in a "lost ethic" such as the Ethic of Reverence for the Dead, and the consequential moral action is vital for any human community to survive, let alone identify the good life.

When invisible and lost ethical teachings and customs totally collapse there is most often an ethical crisis which creates disharmony, confusion and chaos which is not the good life.

Now let us look very hard at thinking, exploring, developing and articulating a standard of principle about the Ethic of Reverence for the Dead and determine if we can further articulate the substance of this ethical principle and describe once again the moral actions which are required to assist people in making an ethical "good" in our actions to care for our sacred dead.

III. THE ETHICAL MODEL OF THE ETHIC OF REVERENCE FOR THE DEAD

Every profession, in order to validate itself, must base that validation upon one primary and supreme ethic. Medicine, for instance, bases its professional practice on the ethic of the Hippocratic Oath which articulates the moral action of healing and health. Law bases its practice on the ethic of truth and justice, and so goes with all professional endeavors.

The basic ethic for the funeral service profession is the Ethic of Reverence for the Dead. This ethic is the bedrock of the human need for death rituals.

It is important that this ethic be developed, analyzed, studied and articulated because it is from this unique and rarely spoken of ethical position that the subsequent psycho-social values of death rites, rituals and ceremonies for the benefit of both the sacred dead and the living has its core.

In the study of general ethics, in order to develop the ethical theory, the student is taught to make intellectual inquiries by formulating and asking a specific type of question about a specific moral topic whatever that subject might be. This is the procedure that is used most often by philosophers to arrive at an absolute objective ethic.

This specific type of question asked in the objective ethical inquiry is called the *"ought/should"* question.

Examples of ought/should questions would be, "What ought we to do about abortion?" or "should war be outlawed?" or "should I pay my taxes when I disagree with how the tax money is being spent?" The specific type of question, this ought/should question begin all objective ethical inquiries. Ought/should questions require a person to think and think deeply; this is not mere opinion making. As the well-respected intellect and Nobel Peace Prize laureate Dr. Albert Schweitzer, said, "All philosophies come from human thought."

The genesis ought/should question for our purposes in developing our absolute ethic is this: "What should we do with the dead?"

For many, without actually thinking about an objective moral position the answer is terribly simple: a person can burn the body or bury the body – that's it – right off the cuff, nice and easy. However, the arduous process required for objective ethical thinking makes clear that no important ethical/moral question is, in the end, that easy to answer. There has never been an absolute objective ethic arrived at by using the "off the cuff" process.

It is from asking this basic ought/should question that all objective ethical inquiries begin. Without intellectual hesitation, ought/should questions are most often large and complicated in content and spectrum, and always reflect and demand hard line thinking and brutal honesty. This is precisely the goal of this book; to objectively as possible define the Ethic of Reverence for the Dead, by asking a specific "ought-should" question and thinking out this very important question out to its logical conclusions.

"What should be done with the dead?" Certainly this specific ethical question is controversial in our complicated contemporary culture. Some would answer this ethical question saying that the dead should be buried. Others would say that the dead should be cremated. Some, of course, would endorse medical school donations and then in our death-denying, death phobic society there are those who would make gallant efforts to avoid the question altogether.

Then there are even those interesting souls who would endorse blasting cremated remains of a loved one out into orbit in a small rocket ship. It appears that the capriciousness of death seems to leave most of us without words; as on the surface, the subject seems to defy logic and clarity, and in consequence sometimes people just give up and answer the question "off the cuff".

It is clear that our beginning ethical question, "What should be done with the dead?" will create many varied opinions. Most times, sadly, these responses reflect innocent people who have not actually given this important ethical question any objective thought. Without people thinking out their ethical position concerning our beginning question, no objective, carefully thought-out ethical position is possible. No objective ethic is ever possible by depending on mere opinions. Deeper thinking and objective truthful analysis of the thinking is warranted.

Naturally these varied opinions concerning this ethical question may well be understandable. However, objective ethical conclusions and, hence, adopted ethical standards of moral attitudes and behaviors stop in their tracks when conclusions are based on opinions, whims, anxieties and prejudices that are not objective. Given the rampant presence of death anxieties and denials in our contemporary culture this hodge-podge of thought is a real possibility – it happens all the time. Death is not a popular topic that many people want to give much thought to let alone develop an objective ethical position concerning.

Ethical confusion arises most times from individual whims, prejudices and anxieties concerning the subject matter and in this state of confused opinions based on prejudices, whims, and anxieties no objective workable ethic is possible. Usually then the quest to define the ethic based on careful, judicious thought is abandoned.

There is a danger in abandoning this ethical inquiry because people get stuck. People get stuck because they continue to hold onto their whims, opinions, and anxieties, exhibiting an exaggerated individualization of the self which declares "If it is my opinion, I am right" "I'm entitled to my own opinion, this is American after all". This is known as subjective morality.

People abandoning this ethic inquiry and holding onto their immature whims and opinions, and hence becoming stuck in a moral freeze is ultimately and eventually challenged by the simple fact that the death rate is 100%. Most people globally, sometime, somewhere, under some type of circumstances will have to face up to this harsh statistic. In the conscious process of abandoning thinking about the subject of death innocent people are vulnerable.

Our task here is much different. Our task in objectively defining the Ethic of Reverence for the Dead is to move beyond confusion based on vulnerable random off the cuff opinion and journey into the realm of the specific objective truth concerning this ethical subject.

We are looking for objective morality.

In order to arrive at this position, we will implement what is called in academic ethics "ethical evaluative criteria." Evaluative criteria are used to organize and systematize our thinking processes and assist in objectively analyzing ethical questions. This academic approach possesses integrity and it is also a safe, systematic way to think about and analyze our subject: Reverence for The Dead. To objectively analyze our ethical questions, the following evaluative criteria will be used:

I.   **HUMAN NATURE**
        This is an examination concerning the basic nature of human beings in reference to the ethical care of dead.

II.   **CONSEQUENCES OF THE ACT**
This is an examination of the history of what has and does happen when people do not ethically take care of the dead.

III.   **UNIVERSAL CONVICTIONS**
This is an examination as to whether or not a basic ethic of reverently caring for the dead is seen in all people and cultures worldwide.

IV.   **MORAL FEELINGS**
This is an examination of how people feel by caring, or by not caring for the dead.

V.   **RELIGIOUS CONVICTIONS AS A GUIDE:**
This is an examination as to whether or not the ethical care of the dead is related to religious principles.

IV. A COMMENTARY CONCERNING THE STATE OF THE SUBJECT OF DEATH AND THE STATUS OF THE DEAD IN MODERN AMERICA

At the outset, it needs to be stated that in Western culture (American culture in particular) human attitudes, in regards to the subjects of death and dying, has progressively since the turn of the 19th century, manifested itself to the point that today there is a pervasive attitude of denial and defiance bordering on phobic.

Talk of death for the 21st century person is avoided even as we stand before the possibility of global annihilation.

Many people erroneously behave in Western contemporary culture as if death has nothing to do with them. This attitude is terribly false for as long as the death rate remains at 100%, all humanity has a tremendous connection to the subjects of death and dying and in particular, our own death.

Death for a human is qualitatively different from other animals; in fact, the human ability of personal death-awareness indicates the fundamental biological difference between human beings and animals.

Death is the most certain event in anyone's biography and also in our present time, the least anticipated.

As long as this cultural climate of death denial continues the Ethic of Reverence for the Dead, the art of preparation and preservation of the dead,

16

and those who work with the dead and who perform this service, will continue to be the subject of controversy. As most contemporary death care professionals, namely funeral directors and embalmers, can readily attest it is a burden to bear and one needs to understand and even be accepting of this current cultural state of affairs.

More specifically, the attitude of the American culture towards death and dying has been for years rooted in avoidance with the subject and the culture as a whole has been extremely successful in this effort. An example of this would be to witness how successful the culture has been in making their burial grounds, their cemeteries look like golf courses.

The current American culture places tremendous value on items that are new, shiny, pretty, expensive, bright and alive. Conversely, American culture devalues and many times shuns the old, the dull, the ugly, the poor, the tired, and, yes, the dead. Given this state of fragile cultural attitudes toward the 100% fact of death, the ethical value of the actual dead body is often morally negated simply because the dead body symbolizes precisely the subject that the culture is in vain trying to avoid – death. As a consequence avoidance with the ultimate symbol of physical death, namely dead bodies, is the consequence.

As will be suggested later, the moral negation of the meaning of just one sacred decedent is one of the cardinal signs of the ethical deterioration of people in a civilized world.

Compounding the complications of this ethical situation is the fact that the dead body in and of itself represents a major psychological and ethical paradox for people. The paradox stems from the fact that psychologically, living people are simultaneously attracted to and repulsed by the vision of the dead. The dead body is the ultimate symbol that represents the reality of physical death, and death remains the ultimate esoteric condition; an experience which humans can never totally explain to satisfaction.

This paradox creates an ethical conundrum which frustrates human beings if they refuse to carefully think out the subject of what it means to ethically care for the dead and their own responsibility concerning the subject.

Much can be said for the wisdom to be had by ethically thinking out what it means for us to care for the dead, and in the process arrive at our own personal connection as to what death actually means in our lives because it is true that the more a person thinks, learns, participates and discerns about death and the actual dead and their own death specifically, the more insights are given on how to live life.

In the human consideration of death valid questions are often times asked, such as "What happened? What does death ultimately mean? What do you think happens after you are dead?"

These are timeless, ancient questions, and when they are asked the human being asking them is in the end ultimately facing a topic which possesses true limits, borders, mysteries and obstacles. It is true we are all going to die, but we can only know so much about the ultimate truth concerning death.

However, no matter how much we learn, what we believe, it is a literal truth that our death is the clearest indication of our finitude, and this is very humbling. This state of affairs many times causes intellectual frustration, and ultimately intellectual defeat. Also many people possess a morbid fear of death; and hence, the subject causes stress and anxieties particularly if it becomes too personal, too close to home.

Ethical thought concerning death, our own death and the care of the dead requires a true sense of authentic humility. Arrogance and death do not go well together.

Since the human does not deal well with defeat or topics that cause anxieties, an elaborate system of denials (which are often very articulate and rational) are set in place to artificially cope with the uncomfortable feelings that death thinking can easily stimulate.

Death is a subject that, if it is not given humble intellectual and moral deference, and resignation, it cannot be embraced or understood. No death lessons can be learned if people do not think about the subject. Death awareness, forming and embracing a mature attitude namely that death is universal, inevitable and irreversible requires careful thought and exploration.

The quick, random, off the cuff response concerning the depth that this moral subject requires is a sure formula for defeat. When this quick random response to death happens, no ethical learning can take place; in this intellectual vacuum the attitude that death has absolutely nothing to do with me takes hold. This attitude does have ethical consequences.

In this atmosphere of denial the stage is set for a morally apathetic attitude towards a basic ethical care of the deceased. It is from the emotionally frustrating position of "I cannot explain what happened," or "It hurts so much that I cannot face it," or "This subject really upsets me and makes me feel really sad and bad" or the intellectually arrogant response "When you're dead, you're dead," or "Roll me over in a ditch when I'm dead" that people turn their intellects and their emotions away from the stark realities of death and, hence, just possibly some of the silent and invisible life lessons that are lurking hidden in the Ethic of Reverence for the Dead.

The denial problem is further compounded and complicated by the fact that there are those today who actually encourage innocent others to regard the dead body as being unimportant and worthless. When the position of denial or apathy concerning the significant ethical value of a dead body succeeds, innocent people deny themselves a valuable therapeutic opportunity. This therapeutic opportunity comes to the living bereaved in the form of a visual and tactile realization that the dead human body image represents, in a symbolic way that a life which was once alive is now dead –

really and truly dead.

Establishing the honest reality of death is a blueprint for each of our respective journeys in life – for no one can live life and not be touched by death, no one.

This type of moral truth opportunity comes only once in life, because a person can only physically die once, and once this reality event is denied and avoided, the ethical and psychological opportunity in recognizing the significance of this event is lost forever. By creating this type of denial of death, in missing the significance of the dead, and in thinking that the dead has nothing to do with me, the groundwork for complicated life experiences is often innocently and unwittingly set. In our society today there are actually seminars being presented which endorse precisely what has been shared in this paragraph. The message of these seminars is this: don't look at the dead. Do what is quick and easy. And lastly that no funeral ritual equals to no grief.

It is ethically unfortunate that such thinking is attractive, but in a culture that denies death, and does it as well as the American culture does, this message is ethically weak, psychologically risky, and untrue. Nonetheless it has become popular by making people feel that they are buffered somehow from the stark realities of the Grim Reaper.

Apathy concerning the significant ethical value of the dead is often extremely subtle making it much harder to detect. The common practice of negating the ethical importance of a dead body through the use of euphemistic cultural jargon to describe the dead, or using humor to laugh at death, and those who represent death in communities is an example of this subtlety. Words and phrases used to describe a deceased human being offer good examples. Words such as "stiff," or "meat," or "the bod," and phrases such as the "Decay Buffet" or "Cadaver City" or the even more creative "Corpses-R-Us" are crude representatives of an unethical and anxious attitude towards the dead and death itself.

Here is another example of the subtle denial of the reality of a human's death: There was a time, not too long ago in fact, when after a patient in the hospital would die the deceased body was permitted by the hospital administration to be reverently removed through the actual front door of the hospital. The dead remains were visibly taken right through the main waiting room of the hospital, and everyone usually bowed their heads, took off their hats, and some even murmured a silent prayer. The ethical message by the moral action was that the now deceased patient had dignity and was revered even in death.

Today when the dead human remains actually leave the medical facility the entrance to the morgue is most often located at the far back end of the hospital next to the garbage dumpster. This practice is not universal, but it is undeniably common in the United States.

In fact, many years ago Dr. Elisabeth Kubler-Ross told me before a seminar in Chicago that when she was preparing to write her 1969 book "On Death and Dying" she went to the Oncology ward at a major hospital in Chicago and asked the head nurse if she could visit dying people, and the head nurse responded, very kindly, "We have no dying patients here."

The Stereotype Stemming From Death Anxiety

Jokes about death, dead bodies, undertakers and cemeteries abound in our culture which reflects the reality of widespread death anxieties. Comments like: "People are dying to get in," or "How's business? A little dead?" are common expressions in the American lexicon.

WAITING FOR A CUSTOMER.

The psychology, of course, motivating such behavior is when a person feels powerless in controlling or even confronting an uncomfortable subject the person so affected reverts to an immature and weak method of staying in control by laughing at and ridiculing the subject. It is difficult to seriously ponder an important life-ethical standard such as the Ethic of Reverence for the Dead when people are laughing at it.

Not only do these crude words, jokes, humor and phrases represent unethical attitudes towards a basic care of the dead, they represent the truth of death anxieties which permeate our culture. More alarming is the fact that our death denying culture is now refining this unethical, anti-corpse language by referring to the dead as a "mass of defunct protoplasm," or the even more imaginative and sophisticated description, " the dead are wasted protein."

It is indeed unfortunate that in our quest for ethical enhancement in reference to a moral reverential care of the dead that this low-culture terminology has found its way into the American vernacular.

V. THE ETHICAL EVALUATIVE CRITERION

ETHICAL CRITERION I – HUMAN NATURE

For one to understand the reason for this apathy in regards to our connection with death, and the subsequent development of denial language in the American culture, we need to examine our developed human nature.

Human nature is indeed a difficult phenomenon to pin down and understand because we are all so different from one another. To help ease this difficulty, an anthropological approach concerning human nature -what is built into us -will be used. This will enable the reader to see that the Ethic of Reverence for the Dead is actually something built into our human nature, into our very being, our instincts; and hence, it becomes an integral part of what may be called more specifically our primal emotive instinct.

Primal emotive instinct is defined here for our purposes as: impulses or powerful motivations which are primal, of first or chief importance, which link us to our ancient ancestors but which can be repressed.

In examining our human nature, or more specifically our primal emotive instincts, we will focus on the Neanderthal period of development and focus on what use this early group made of their dead. What is referred to as the ethical or reverential care of the dead was first discovered in the instinctive behavior of the Neanderthal. It is this instinctive behavior and actions associated that show and elaborate the beginning of the primal emotive instinct which people, to this day, still possess in their inner resources to morally care for the dead.

The culture and the emotional sophistications and complications of the Neanderthal's world were simple but extremely brutal – life was fragile, and dangerous; death was visible, all the time, everywhere. The Neanderthal had no choice but to listen inwardly to his feelings and instincts for there existed no sophisticated alternatives when it came to dealing with their dead. It was through this process of listening and then acting upon feelings and instincts that the Neanderthal set the original, built-in human nature to ethically care for the dead. The Neanderthal did this naturally by implementing all sorts of rites, rituals, and ceremonies to surround the significant event of the death of one of their own.

Anthropological research indicates that human burial is among the oldest of all customs, and has been known from c.62000 B.C. among the Homo sapiens neanderthanlensis (Neanderthal). This evidence was discovered in the Shanidar Cave in 1952 by Dr. Ralph Solecki (1917 -) in Northern Iraq.

In the Shanidar Cave, Dr. Solecki and his anthropological researchers discovered seven corpses which all had been covered with the hard bone of large animal bone. The decedents had all been placed in the fetal position and covered with red clay earth. It clearly appeared that attempts to replicate the cycle from birth to death had been implemented. It was a kind of life cycle symbol that these primitives were attempting.

Also found around the corpses were flower pollen fragments. It has been determined that the oldest ethical funeral tribute, the oldest form of death rites, rituals and ceremonies and the oldest act of mourning is the arrangement and placement of flowers around the dead.

Dr. Solecki during his famous archeological dig at Shanidar submitted soil samples from each grave to Arlette Leroi-Gourhan (1913 – 2005), a paleobotanist from Paris, France for pollen analysis. She found under her microscope pollen and flower fragments from at least eight species of flowers. These flowers represented mainly small brightly colored wild flowers. She recognized floral relatives of the grape hyacinth, bachelor's-button, hollyhock, and the yellow-flowering groundsel.

Mme Leroi-Gourhan declared that it was no accident of nature that the flower pollen was deposited so deep in the cave. Also, neither birds nor animals could have carried flowers in such a manner in the first place and in the second place, they could not possibly have deposited them directly square on top of a burial site. Therefore, she concluded that people 62,000 years ago had roamed the mountainside in the mournful task of collecting flowers to be used in rites, rituals and ceremonies whereby they could express their grief.

To connect the built-in Ethic of Reverence for the Dead with human nature we can easily link the ancient with the present in that people to this very day still use flowers as memorial tributes. This, then, is a primary example of our built in ethical and moral propensity to  care for our dead through attention and action which is built into our primal instincts. It is our human nature to act and to do something when death occurs.

The inward process of uncomplicated listening that Neanderthal did so spontaneously is a good example of our primal emotive instinct. It is within this ethical instinctive tendency, which humans still possess to this very day, that the rudiments of the genesis of rites, rituals, and ceremonies exist. However, in the 21st century this instinct to act and do something when someone dies can easily be repressed.

Today by simply being attentive to our own primal emotive instinct, contemporary people have within them an excellent vehicle of knowledge and a moral barometer that instructs them as to their moral and ethical options and obligations to care for the dead in a reverent manner. However, this instinct - the moral barometer - requires human action for the Ethic of Reverence for the Dead to live and possess effectiveness in bettering human life and the experience of loss and grief.

Interestingly, small children who have little factual knowledge of the world but have unlimited feeling capacities about life, have no choice but to listen inwardly on how to act. By simply listening to their feeling even these small children will instinctively bury a dead pet if they are left to their own devices. If adults do not interfere and stop their acts small children possess the capacity to very creatively use rites, rituals and ceremonies in response to special significant events in their life; this act is called play.

The rabbit's burial.

Neanderthal's ancient world, as in the world of the child, there clearly neither existed nor exist denials or rationalizations about the reality of the significant events in life. The death of someone in the tribe simply happened or the death of a pet simply happened for the child; it was and is a fact of life. Both responded by recognizing the significance of the event and used what was at their disposal to embrace the event – namely rites, rituals and ceremony.

Today however, the reality of death is still just as valid and just as true but this reality and truth has been fiddled with and repressed. Adults have the ability to repress and deny, it is sometimes referred to as the "games people play". The repression and hence rejection of the stark realities of death has risen steadily over the last century, particularly in the West.

Burial of the pet bird, by E.C. Rideout.

It is very interesting that just a short century ago people could and did talk about death nonstop. Death was everywhere all the time, it was extremely visible.

People died at home with everybody, even little children witnessing the death. Embalming was done in the family home. Funerals were held out of the family home with little children routinely in attendance.

Volumes of poetry and verse was written and recited as forms coping and of entertainment about death. William Cullen Bryant's famous death poem "Thanatopsis" and his frequent recitation of the poem was the "rock star" event of the Victorian era in the United States. In fact, Mr. Bryant traveled the country giving recitations of his poem. The contents of "Thanatopsis" taught the audiences clear lessons about the reality and consequences of the death of just one human being. Death was a highly visible part of Victorian life, and the Ethic of Reverence for the Dead was alive and well.

But sex, how babies got here, how life is created, that was a different thing altogether 100 years ago. Adults told children things about how babies got into the world that even the adult's themselves did not believe. Sex was taboo, and there were ethical consequences for the culture that acted as if sex had nothing to do with them (unwanted pregnancies were common in 1900).

It is an interesting social observation that in just 100 short years the subjects of death and sex in American culture have literally flip-flopped, and

death has come out, ethically speaking, on the short end of the stick; death is now the taboo subject.

Moral flip-flopping which we see so prevalent in American attitudes today towards death and sex was not an option for the ancient world of the Neanderthal. Hence, the ethical and ceremonial response to death of a member of their group was that Neanderthals proceeded in an ethical, although primitive manner to express care and reverence for the deceased. Neanderthals exemplified the beginning ethical behaviors which had become part of the characteristic of our developed human nature in ethical relations to a reverential care for the dead. However, in present times this ethical position has been eroded.

The Neanderthal was not bombarded with all sorts of advice as to how they should or should not react and behave. Neanderthals did not have access to "how to" seminars. No "pop" psychology existed in Neanderthal's world; no TV people were telling the Neanderthal what to do and how to do it. There simply existed the pure primal emotive instinct to care for the dead by doing something. When death occurred, this primal emotive instinct clicked in, and very sincere preparations were made for the disposition of a dead person which included amongst other things floral tributes. That genetic and instinctive legacy remains with us and in us today tempered by culture and intellect. This is a primitive example of the Ethic of Reverence for the Dead transforming itself into primitive moral activities.

Of additional interest in our exploration of the notion of "instinct" and its relationship to the ethic is the growing awareness that animals with large brains engage in and do respond when the death of a member of the herd or group dies. For instance, dolphin mothers may refuse to part with the dead bodies of their babies who die, even forgoing food and tirelessly keeping their dead children buoyant in the water day after day.

Jane Goodall famously reported that a chimpanzee juvenile, even though mature enough to feed on his own, could not recover emotionally from the death of his mother, and soon died himself.

While these examples are compelling it is in the social attachments and behaviors of elephants that the instinctual power to care for the dead is clearly recognized. Mother elephants who lose offspring of any age mourn for them. Their grief is displayed physically by sunken eyes and drooping ears. When a member of the herd dies elephants search for and gathers leaves and twigs. They then bring them back to the dead body and use them to cover it. Elephants have also been observed revisiting the site where a member of their family or herd died even years afterward, just as a human might do.

The British zoologist Ian Douglas-Hamilton OBE, who started an organization called "Save the Elephants" has recorded scores of elephant grief behaviors. The following account was taken from a National Geographic assignment that Dr. Douglas-Hamilton was on:

"The dying cow sinks to her haunches as members of the herd form a protective semi-circle about her. With a large convulsion the cow heaves to her side, and dies. One bull remains beside her and tries repeatedly to lift the cow to her feet. Other elephants put their trunks into the cow's mouth, and push against her again and again. The bull of the herd trumpets loud and long, and finally he attempts to mount her, as if he had tried every behavior he could think of and in desperation he had turned to sex. The elephants stayed with the dead cow for several hours, as if they could not immediately adjust to the finality of her death. After ten days the corpse was rotten and the herd returned. They sniffed cautiously at first. The tusks of the dead cow were the cause of excited interest, and eventually the tusks of the dead cow were taken with the herd.

- DR. IAIN DOUGLAS-HAMILTON

Given that the human being possesses the largest brain on earth we should not be in anyway surprised at or detoured from the realization that humans can develop and implement the most sophisticated methods of ethically caring for their dead on earth. It is built into us.

The grieving responses and activities of elephants.

ETHICAL CRITERION II – CONSEQUENCES OF THE ACT

This section of the text will examine the consequences of being unethical or irreverent in a basic ethical care for the sacred dead.

Centuries ago, even just 100 years ago, the care of the dead and the subject of death was extremely important. The great theologians and philosophers of the day intellectualized and thought deeply about the subject of death. As this intellectual pondering about death went forward, the world was given many answers to questions concerning death.

So encompassing and influential was this philosophical contemplation of death that one of the common denominators in the results of such magnanimous efforts of thought is that what many of the world's religious thinkers have in common; they address and attempt to give education, lessons, and answers to the living about human death, and most particularly answers to just what happens to a person after they die.

This clearly indicates then that there was a time when the subject of death, physical death (not human grief), and the care of dead bodies commanded much attention. From this intellectual thought the Ethic of Reverence for the Dead was developed, recognized and practiced.

Unfortunately there was an accompanying dark side to this high level thinking and pondering. Often the answers which were promoted and arrived at by the philosophers about death created just as many wide interpretations than the questions did. Many answers concerning the meaning, nature and effect of death on the living ended up creating human superstitions and morbid fears which made the dead body, being the tangible symbol of death, a taboo, a source of fear, possessed of evil spirits, an object of avoidance and something unclean.

While the dead during this historic period of antiquity were certainly used in rites, rituals and ceremonies, a basic attitude of fear and apprehension emerged, gone was the tribal innocence of centuries past. From these superstitious attitudes came the horror stories of ghosts, the living dead and charnel houses (these were places in churches in Europe where the dead were actually hung on hooks and hung from the interior walls of the sanctuary, this was terribly obnoxious to the living).

It was at this critical juncture in the historic development of human thought concerning the people's relationships with the dead that the dead started to be problematic and the source of fearful anxieties.

Sadly many of these meaningless medieval and antiquated superstitions concerning dead human beings still persist today, making the work of the individuals whose work and career in actually dealing with the sacred dead much more difficult.

Many contemporary people continue to hold to the fallacy that the dead are somehow unclean and that the people who devote their lives to maintaining the Ethic of Reverence for the Dead by caretaking of the actual dead are somehow strange, odd and different.

It is important for us to see that under the canopy of superstitious and anxious thought concerning the dead, the living began to disengage themselves from a reverential care of the dead, both in action and attitude. This tendency has only grown over the last century. This historical-evolutionary process of the deterioration of the Ethic of Reverence for the Dead and its consequences can clearly be seen when one examines certain governmental and sociological declines in world history.

When the reverential, ethical care of the dead is not held as being of high ethical importance, one can see in world history that the destruction of famous civilizations was, in part, heralded by an unspoken yet highly visible rise in a community's moral apathy concerning the ethical care of their dead.

The apathetic attitude that ancient Roman citizens held concerning a basic care of their dead was commonplace as Rome was finally sacked and destroyed. The Roman attitude in its final chapter in history saw the reverential moral act of caring for the dead replaced by the celebratory attitude of eat, drink and be merry. Ancient Greece experienced a similar fate, and common practice in both civilizations at the end of their history was a widespread ignoring of the reality and significance of physical death which was replaced by a caviler, carefree, blissful approach to living life. The result being that irreverent care of the dead was common place, which contributed, amongst other reasons for the collapse of these powerful civilizations.

However, we do not have to return to the ancient history of long-gone powerful civilizations like Rome and Greece to see the utter and disastrous consequences that can happen to a nation and civilization that allows the Ethic of Reverence for the Dead to evaporate and vanish.

Nazi death camps – the epitome of violating the Ethic of Reverence for the Dead.

In modern times, in the lifetime of many who are still living, from basically 1933 to 1945 the Nazi German Nation created morally haunting and repulsive places with names like Belsen, Auschwitz-Birenau, Chelmno, Sobibor and Treblinka. These places, and hundreds more like them, remain in our collective memory as sobering reminders and dramatic examples of the catastrophic danger inherent in a people abandoning the Ethic of Reverence for the Dead. Today even the mere mention of the German concentration camps creates revulsion and is ethically repugnant to morally sensitive and thinking people. The collapse of the developed Ethic of Reverence for the Dead, in this example, tragically translated into reprehensible moral actions by human beings, which in turn was a contributing factor to the collapse of the Nazi culture and morals. It is interesting to note that those rare freethinkers during this insane period of history who stood up for the wisdom of the ethic, and, who stood on moral grounds refusing to participate in the wholesale slaughter of millions of the sacred living and also the irreverent care of millions of the sacred dead, were faced with their own executions.

The unfortunate fate of these rare freethinkers who stood up to defend the Ethic of Reverence for the Dead and the Ethic of Reverence for Life (although they did not call it precisely these names) is a good example and lesson as to just what possibly can be the consequences of taking a high absolute moral stance concerning an ethical subject.

Absolute moral actions always require moral courage.

The moral history lesson is undisputable: Toward the end of each of these powerful national examples, the irreverent care of the dead was commonplace. Given this historical information, this ethical and moral question begs to be asked: What happened to these civilizations that let irreverent care of the dead happen? Time and again the annals of history show that the repetitive methods of rites, rituals and ceremonies based on ethical thinking and moral actions surrounding the dead are excellent barometers to indicate basic civilization levels and attainments a people have reached or the lack thereof.

William Ewart Gladstone
1809 - 1898

The eminent British Prime Minister William Ewart Gladstone articulated this ethical position very well when he wrote:

"Show me the manner in which a nation or community cares for its dead and I will measure with mathematical exactness the tender sympathies of its people, their respect for the Laws of the Land, and their loyalty to High ideals."

In our fast-paced contemporary society, we might ponder seriously what Gladstone is saying and time-out might well be in order so tough questions can be asked, such as: What is our present day tender sympathies for each other? What is our present day respect for the laws of the land? What is people's present day loyalty to high ideals? Finally, what are we doing with our sacred dead and how are the sacred dead being treated?

The unmistakable present trends of abandoning the importance of the sacred dead human body as an **essential** focus of part of the grief experience in rites, rituals and ceremonies can be traced to a steady deterioration of the larger ethical ideal of a civilization. This is precisely what Mr. Gladstone is referring to in magnifying the ethical care for the sacred decedent.

The great American thinker Benjamin Franklin (1706 – 1790) put this ethical sentiment of Gladstone's linking the living to the dead another way.

> *"In order for me to understand a community all I have to do is visit their cemetery."*

ETHICAL CRITERION III – UNIVERSAL CONVICTIONS

The ethical question in this ethical criterion called Universal Convictions is this: Is it valid to maintain that all cultures everywhere on the face of the earth morally act and express and reflect the Ethic of Reverence for the Dead by their developed rites, rituals and ceremonies which are common to all and understood by all? Is there evidence that attests to the fact that reverential care of the dead is a universal moral conviction that is valued in all cultures across the globe?

Consider the following well established cultural universals in reference to the reverential care of the dead:

I.   It is a well-documented fact in all anthropological, archaeological and comparative religious studies and literature that every culture and civilization ever studied has used and continues to use the structural form of rites, rituals and ceremonies, with the dead body present, to help the community assimilate the larger-than-life experience of death. While the variety of these rites, rituals and ceremonies take on every conceivable form, nonetheless the Ethic of Reverence for the Dead can morally be witnessed and documented by people's actions. There are few global examples of where the dead human body does not take an essential position in death rites, rituals and ceremonies, and no examples of where death rituals do not exist. However, there is one glaring exception:

31

One place where the trend of eliminating the dead human body as an essential in death rites, rituals and ceremonies is in the United States of America.

In contrast are the rites, rituals and ceremonies in New Zealand, the United Kingdom and Ireland. In these cultures the sacred decedent is a prominent essential in their ceremonial activities and ritualistic meaning. While their cremation rate is very high, interestingly their rate of cremation with no death ritual or ceremony is extremely low. In addition, residential/home funerals are a common practice.

II. Every culture, every civilization ever studied or documented as to its death customs maintains sacred places where the bodies and relics of their dead are placed (i.e. a cemetery, mausoleum, columbarium, church, etc.) The moral action evidence of the power of the Ethic of Reverence for the Dead can be seen by the utter horror of communities when their sacred burial sites are vandalized. In warfare, it is a much-used morale destroyer for the conquering nation to tear down and destroy the conquered countries sacred burial sites; for nothing can deflate and defeat the moral identity and moral fiber of a conquered people more than to have their sacred burial sites destroyed. This is another example of just how powerful the moral consequences are when the ethic is abused, ignored, or worse; the very significance of its meaning is not even recognized.

III. Every culture, every civilization ever studied, pre-literate or literate, attests to human expressions of the Ethic of Reverence for the Dead through endless examples of art, music and literature that help to maintain a continuance from generation to generation of the meaning and lessons of reverence for the dead. These are powerful examples of human moral action. For instance, art examples of funerary art monuments/memorials would be: The Lincoln Memorial, The Tomb of the Unknown Soldier, The tomb of Dr. Martin Luther King, Jr. Westminster Abbey. Examples of music would be: Requiem masses of

Mozart, Brahms, Verdi, old-time funeral hymns such as, "In the Garden", and "The Old Rugged Cross". Literature such as: Allen Tate's poem "Ode to the Confederate Dead" or T.S. Eliot's "The Hollow Men" and plays such as Shakespeare "King Lear" and "Antigone" by Sophocles, and even Arthur Miller's "Death of a Salesman".

One of the most poignant artistic examples of music in expressing the Ethic of Reverence for the Dead was witnessed when Eric Clapton's composed the touching song "Tears in Heaven" after the death of his son, who was killed by falling out of a window. This piece of music was a morally noble action and successful effort to express the pain of grief of this unfathomable tragedy, and artistically captured the ethic.

By using these three sub-criteria (art, music, literature) we can see that literally thousands of examples could be used to show how diverse and widespread the human moral customs are and responses and peoples creativity in rituals attempting to express actions toward fulfilling a basic ethical reverential care of the dead. In fact, the universal presence and historic impact of the Ethic of Reverence for the Dead is so massive that no one publication could possibly document all the various customs, and rites, rituals and ceremonies concerning death that exist on a global basis.

All the world-wide funeral customs (morality in action) surrounding death finds their origins and roots in the ethic; it motivates moral action on the part of human beings. Without the ethic or by rationally dismissing the significance of this ethic, the customs and rituals that we have developed over the ages of time become a nuisance, then a burden, which in short time means the rituals become meaningless, and the moral action collapses. Nothing is more morally, theologically and spiritually depleting to the human soul than to participate in rites, rituals and ceremonies that have no meaning. Meaninglessness is always the death sentence for any rite, ritual or ceremony.

ETHICAL CRITERION IV – MORAL FEELINGS

Ethical criterion number four asks the question as to whether a person will emotionally feel right, wrong or indifferent by caring or by not caring in an ethically reverential manner for a dead person.

The issue of moral feelings in reference to reverential care of the dead comes to confronting the issue of logic versus emotions. Our rational logic may well dismiss the corpse as a "mass of defunct protein," but one's emotions will often set up barriers which may well lead to an internal collision and conflict between logic and emotions. This internal ethical collision process is of no small importance. It is precisely when we feel this collision of logic versus emotions that we should realize that our deep primal emotive instincts are beckoning to us for recognition. This is something that is felt. This type of collision process may be referred to as our internal moral checkpoint or compass. In other words, the collision of logic versus emotions serves as a jolt for us to listen, precisely as Neanderthals did, to our inward emotions and avoid getting caught up in the denial, reductionism and rationalization trap.

President Kenney in State

To illustrate the process by which our primal emotive moral checkpoints surface, we will examine a relatively unknown chapter in death care history in the United States. The year was 1963 and this particular year was one of profound change for the funeral service profession. The publication of Jessica Mitford's (1917 – 1996) book *The American Way of Death* created one of the most savage and relentless attacks ever targeted on the funeral service profession. Miss Mitford launched attacks against and criticized American funeral practices and funeral directors. She was not bashful in accusing all funeral directors of being thieves, merchants of sorrow, and immoral crooks. Miss Mitford used death humor to laugh at funeral directors, and, therefore; laugh at death as funeral directors are a living symbol of the reality of death in most every community. As a result of her publication, Miss Mitford was herself the target of a counter defense by the funeral directors. It unfortunately was a type of siege mentality, and both sides seemed pitted against each other until November 22, 1963.

The death and subsequent funeral of President John F. Kennedy rocked an entire nation's moral checkpoint of primal emotive instincts. People did not consciously know why, but it no longer felt right to criticize a group or read negative things about the group (the funeral directors) who now symbolized death and funerals in a big way. The nation's population was intimately involved in a very significant death and funeral process composed of rites, rituals and ceremonies, and, yes, where the Ethic of Reverence for the Dead was seen by millions of everyday people on television. The result of people strongly feeling this ethic was that Mitford's book sales plummeted.

Upon the death of President Kennedy the issue of logic versus emotions suddenly seemed unimportant. People were glued to watching the rituals that reflected the impact of the Ethic of Reverence for the Dead.

It would have been socially repulsive and ethically unacceptable for President Kennedy's body to have been described as "wasted protein," or a "stiff" or worse, disposed of without any rites, rituals or ceremonies, without the ethic being present in moral human action.

It was the Ethic of Reverence for the Dead that made its moral impact on millions of people worldwide who felt, without being able to articulate it, the moral truth and impact concerning just how deeply this ethic was a part of the Kennedy funeral experience.

However, we cannot depend on the assassination of our nation's leaders to teach people these moral lessons. As funeral professionals we are the moral guardians of this ethic, and, hence, it is our responsibility to speak and teach about it. If funeral professionals do not stand up and defend this important vital ethical position, who will?

It is a moral obligation.

Moral feelings which represent our primal emotive instincts to ethically and reverently care for the dead surface under other conditions also. For example communities and families are distraught beyond verbal description when and if a dead body is missing or worse never found. Thousands of taxpayers' dollars are spent in recovery and search efforts, and there are community signs of high anxiety and remorse when such recovery efforts fail.

Of course based upon logic alone, or reducing these search and recovery efforts to money, or if we accept the notion that the dead body is of no value and has no meaning to us, then these magnanimous search and recovery efforts make little, if any, sense and could actually be seen as a waste of the tax payers dollars! Aren't these missing individuals dead? Aren't they "a mass of defunct protoplasm?" Missing in action relatives can quickly and sincerely articulate the vital importance of the Ethic of The Reverence for the Dead by simply sharing their life experience.

John F. Kennedy, Jr. was killed when his plane crashed in the ocean.

When the dead human remains of Mr. Kennedy, his wife and occupants in the plane were recovered, the Kennedy family instructed the funeral professionals that the deceased were to be cremated and scattered in the ocean. Some people questioned the why and wherefore of such a decision. The position they morally took was something like: "They were already dead in the water!" or "How much did that cost?" or "That is stupid!" Such a moral attitude from an ethical perspective is truly limited, and worse, offensive to our ethical and emotional sensibilities, and morally insensitive.

It was the Ethic of Reverence for the Dead that motivated the grieving Kennedy family to make every moral effort to bring their loved ones home and when that fact was accomplished and assured (whether this made logical sense or not) the Kennedy family implemented rites, rituals, and ceremonies and morally and ethically disposed of their dead in a legal manner and according to their religious convictions.

Imagine the ethical horror if portions of the dead from this tragic accident washed ashore on some island around Massachusetts. The reaction would have been appalling for the simple reason that the ethic and respect for the dead would have been violated.

However the ethic was not violated by magnanimous efforts on the part of the living to recover the sacred dead; in this instance, the Ethic of Reverence for the Dead was in free moral action, and fulfilling the ethic eventually gave to the mourning family participants the feeling that they had morally done the right thing, which in bereavement care is a priceless gift to possess.

When there is no sacred decedent, logic suddenly becomes secondary, as the families of people declared missing in action in a war can readily attest. When there is no corpse, something of extreme ethical value is missing; moral action is stymied. An important piece of the realistic bereavement puzzle is gone. Something essential is missing and no replacement accessory can equally substitute. When there is no sacred decedent the ideal purity of the Ethic has been corrupted and the moral actions of people are many times frozen.

People's moral feelings concerning the Ethic of Reverence for the Dead surface also through the attempts we make as people in remembering our dead in the design, construction and erection of memorials and monuments. The American culture may well deny and defy death in a literal sense, but our culture does, millions of times each year, allow our primal emotive instincts, our human nature, to express our feelings concerning respect for the dead to morally surface through our memorials. Washington, Lincoln, Jefferson, Mt. Rushmore, the World War II Memorial, The Dr. Martin Luther King, Jr. Memorial, the Tomb of the Unknown Soldier, every country cemetery, and every columbarium is a real attempt to express this basic built-in predisposition to ethically care for the dead. Monument designing and construction is a highly visible evidence of the Ethic of Reverence for the Dead in moral action.

Visiting Westminster Abbey, or the Cemetery at Normandy, or the Necropolis in Glasgow, or the National Cemetery of the Pacific in Honolulu or the Papal Crypts at the Vatican or the final resting places in a forest or ocean when cremated remains have been scattered, or the simple country cemetery are all glaring examples of the power of the ethic and the resulting moral creative activities of human beings.

It is valuable to mention once again that in warfare the greatest insult that a conquering nation can give to the conquered nation is the destruction of their sacred burial places. Nothing can demoralize people quicker. Every day communities are morally outraged and angered and depressed when vandals attack their sacred burial grounds or ransack their cremation columbarium's. Our monuments and burial sites are extremely important to us. The strength of this moral importance is a cardinal reflection of the power of the Ethic of Reverence for the Dead.

The power of this ethic is so strong that in the instance of the Tomb of the Unknown Soldier, people can gather and make the ethic come alive even in the instance of a dead person that has no formal identity and that no one personally knows. However, in living the depth of the ethic is so profound that people do know the identity of the Unknown Soldier – because morally and symbolically the soldiers name is Freedom, Liberty, Republic, Honor, Duty, and Country. This is the power of the Ethic of Reverence for the Dead.

Neanderthals made memorials using hard bone of large animals and flowers. Today the modern person uses granite and marble and flowers. The built-in ethical and moral action is precisely the same. All that is different today is the materials that are used. These very observable moral tendencies validate the fact that the human being has a built-in system to ethically care for the dead. It is part of the human experience of being moral beings.

ETHICAL CRITERION V –
RELIGIOUS HERITAGE AS A GUIDE
(*The Judeo-Christian Tradition*)

The next ethical criterion for examination is using religious thinking as a guide in our quest to further define the Ethic of Reverence for the Dead.

This criterion is important to consider, for the funeral ritual in Judaism and Christianity, as well as for a host of other world religions has been, for centuries, essentially a religious ritual. This commentary will be limited to focus upon the Judeo-Christian tradition by virtue of the fact that the majority of Western death customs have originated from this heritage. Certainly, commentaries of great length and great worth could be made concerning the ethical and morally reverential care of the dead in other world religions, but unfortunately time and space do not permit that type of investigation.

In establishing whether or not God has revealed any ethical standards and moral action guides which are to be practiced in the ethical care for the dead, one must start at the written source, The Old Testament and the New Testament.

In the Old Testament, the dead are viewed as being unclean. It is through the specific rites of purification that one who cares for the dead becomes clean again. The Biblical purification process is important, for from the beginning, Biblical references to caring for the dead and the procedures that are to be followed in accomplishing this task (rites of purification, burial procedures, etc.) have been specific in nature and translate into moral action. For example:

Genesis 23:1-20 – Sarah Dies and Abraham Buys a Burial Ground

Sarah lived to be 127 years old. She died in Hebron in the land of Canaan, and Abraham mourned her death.

"He (Abraham) left the place where his wife's body was lying, went to the Hittites, and said, "I am a foreigner living here among you; sell me some land, so that I can bury my wife."

They answered, "Listen to us, sir. We look upon you as a mighty leader, bury your wife in the best grave that we have. Any of us would be glad to give you a grave, so that you can bury her. Then Abraham bowed before them and said, "If you are willing to let me bury my wife here, please ask Ephron son of Zohar to sell me Machpelah Cave, which is near the edge of his field. Ask him to sell it to me for its full price, here in your presence, so that I can own it as a burial ground."

Ephron himself was sitting with the other Hittites at the meeting place at the city gate. He answered in the hearing of everyone there, "Listen, sir: I will give you the whole field and the cave that is in it. Here in the presence of my own people, I will give it to you, so that you can bury your wife.

The Burial of Sarah

But Abraham bowed before the Hittites and said to Ephron, so that everyone could hear, "May I ask you, please, to listen. I will buy the whole field. Accept my payment, and I will bury my wife there."

Ephron answered, "Sir, land worth only four hundred pieces of silver – what is that between us? Bury your wife in it. Abraham agreed and weighed out the amount that Ephron had mentioned in the hearing of the people – four hundred pieces of silver, according to the standard weights used by the merchants.

That is how the property which had belonged to Ephron at Machpelah east of Mamre became Abraham's. It included the field, the cave which was in it, and all the trees in the field up to the edge of the property. It was recognized as Abraham's property by all the Hittites who were there at the meeting.

Then Abraham buried his wife Sarah in that cave in the land of Canaan. So the field which had belonged to the Hittites, and the cave in it, became the property of Abraham for a burial ground.

Comments

When Sarah, wife of the great Old Testament patriarch Abraham, died in Hebron in the land of Canaan, Abraham proposed to the Hittites that he buy from them, land suitable for a burying ground.

Considering Abraham a great prince among them, the Hittites offered him the use of their own choicest burial sepulchers for free, but Abraham declined their gift. Out of reverence and love for his wife Sarah, Abraham insisted on **buying** burial property. This was a moral action.

A man named Ephron had burial land at the Cave of Machpelah near Mamre. Abraham decided this would be the final resting place for his dead wife Sarah. The Cave of Machpelah was to serve as the last resting place of most of the patriarchs: Abraham, Isaac, and Jacob. The site (probably authentic) can still be visited in Hebron to this day. The significance of Machpelah was that it was Abraham's - he owned it, and thus was Israel's first territorial holding in Canaan.

Ephron was also a great admirer of Abraham and wanted to give him the burial site. Again Abraham declined on the moral ground of needing to own his wife's final resting place. Finally, he succeeded in paying about 400 shekels of silver (worth about $250.00) for the burial site. In this family plot Sarah was laid to rest; and later Rebekah and Leah were to be interred there.

Abraham made clear the moral mandate (for his ethical standard) of purchasing the burial site.

This ancient example of the Ethic of Reverence for the Dead contributed in a large way to the historic and moral acceptance in action of both Jewish and Christian burial rites, rituals and ceremonies for the last 5000 years. It is an impressive moral legacy for humanity today.

Genesis 50:1-3

In the Old Testament specific reference to embalming is made twice. First, in Genesis 50: 2-3 is given Jacob's death account. Here is described the embalming care that Jacob's son, Joseph, commanded:

"And Joseph commanded his servants, the physicians, to embalm his father. So the physicians embalmed Israel."

"Joseph threw himself on his father, crying and kissing his face. Then Joseph gave orders to embalm his father's body. It took forty days, the normal time for embalming. The Egyptians mourned him for seventy days.

Comments

It is well known that the ancient Egyptians were experts at embalming. In their own religious concepts it was for the journey to the world of the dead, but in Jacob's case it was no less appropriate for the long funeral cortege to Palestine.

There was tremendous moral meaning associated with the human need to return Jacob's dead human body to Palestine. In this instance specific preparation of the sacred remains was required so the body would not be unduly offensive for the completion of this critically important pilgrimage; the account of which altered the course of world history.

The preparation of Jacob's dead body was an ancient example of the Ethic of Reverence for the Dead, in that the purpose of the treatment was so that Jacob's remains could be taken on the trip to the Promised Land. It would have been far easier to bury the body of Jacob near the place where he died, but the ethic of caring for his sacred dead body, and the love that the bereaved had for the body of Jacob, morally demanded and then inspired and motivated them to moral action, and to make their final decision of what to do on other factors, not based on mere logic, convenience or ease. They made a moral decision.

In 2nd Samuel, Saul has died. King David is commanded by God to go up to the city of Hebron in Judah. While dwelling in the city of Hebron, the men of Jabesh Gilead of Judah, who had buried the body of Saul, are sent for by King David.

"The men of Judah came, and there they anointed David King over the house of Judah. And they told David saying, 'The men of Jabesh Gilead were the ones who buried Saul.' So David sent a messenger to the men of Jabesh Gilead, and said to them, 'You are blessed of the Lord, for you have shown this kindness to your Lord, to Saul, and have buried him.'" (2nd Samuel 2:4-5)

Comments

Throughout the ages of time, certain people have been given or assigned the difficult task of morally and professionally taking care of the dead.

In 2nd Samuel King David blesses the men of Jabesh Gilead who buried Saul (who actively undertook this moral task). These individuals were a living example of exercising the Ethic of Reverence for the Dead through the moral action of caring for the dead.

The Apocryphal Book of Tobit and the Ethic of Reverence for the Dead

In the books of certain Bibles there is an included section known as the Apocrypha and in this section one finds the *Book of Tobit.* (Note: The Apocrypha is not in all editions of the Holy Scriptures).

This book tells the story of a righteous Israelite of the Tribe of Naphtali named **Tobit** living in Nineveh after the deportation of the northern tribes of Israel to Assyria in 721 BC. Tobit is particularly noted for his moral diligence in attempting to provide proper burials for fallen Israelites who have been slain.

In the tradition of the Roman Catholic Church, which includes the Apocrypha, the Book of Tobit doctrinally is cited often for its teaching on three spiritual attributes: the intercession of angels, humble piety, and **Reverence for the Dead.** In the Roman Catholic tradition there are seven Corporal Acts of Mercy, and the seventh and final Corporal Act of Mercy is to bury the dead. In contemporary society the funeral professional is the moral custodian of this professional ethical standard and principle.

The New Testament

Turning now to the New Testament, one finds additional references which further reflect the time honored Judeo-Christian ethical tradition to reverently and morally care for the dead.

MARK 6:27-29 we read of the execution of John the Baptist.

"And immediately the King sent an executioner and commanded his (John the Baptist's) head to be brought. And he went and beheaded him in prison, brought his head on a platter, and gave it to the girl and the girl gave it to her mother. And when his disciples heard of it they came and took away his corpse and laid it in a tomb." (Mark 6:27-29)

Comments

In this Biblical account we see the active moral standard that the corpse is taken away and that the body of John the Baptist is reverentially laid in a tomb. The writer of Mark may well have dismissed the body of John as being morally unimportant, but this was not the case. The disciples were sent to reverently and, with exercising moral action, bring John's body to the tomb. This moral action took effort and time on the part of the disciples and clearly indicates that this period in antiquity placed great importance on the ethical care of the martyred dead. Throughout the Scriptures the Ethic of Reverence for the Dead is of paramount importance.

Interestingly in Biblical times the manner in which a deceased person was buried was very important as to the level of moral admiration and respect that the deceased had held in the community. For instance upon Jezebel's death (2 Kings 9:30 – 37) her dead body was not viewed as morally significant (because of her history and behaviors) and was given to the dogs in the streets to be devoured after her death.

JOHN 11:44

In the Book of John the Lazarus story offers further accounts in reference to the absolute moral teachings in the Judeo-Christian tradition to reverently and morally care for the dead. From a funeral service perspective, the Lazarus story gives the description of actual burial preparations which implement the Ethic of Reverence for the Dead. This scripture describes moral burial practices in caring for the dead which are still being observed to this very day by certain Jewish religious sects in their sacred preparations for human burial. In John 11:44 we read:

"And he who had died came out bound hand and foot with grave straps, and his face was wrapped with cloth. Jesus said to them, "'Loose him and let him go.'"

The use of grave straps may seem a minor point, but indeed in reference to a developing historical ethic to morally care for the dead the process of binding the corpse was and is very important and is still strictly observed in certain Jewish sects. The ethical point is this: Lazarus was not irreverently disposed of; instead Lazarus was morally cared for in a manner that has continued to this very day in Jewish funeral and burial customs and which was passed on through history. By the careful use of grave straps binding Lazarus's arms, feet and chin, his sacred dead body was morally positioned by living human beings into a normal lifelike appearance and made ready for easy handling during the required transportation to the burial site. This process of binding the corpse took time and effort on the part of the living, and this is one of the moral core values of the Ethic of Reverence for the Dead. It is the moral decisions which are made by the living which ultimately set the standards of ethical observance in caring for the dead, or the lack thereof. Dead people cannot take care of themselves; they require moral attention from the living. Morally speaking, just because you are dead, does not mean you are not still a sacred human being.

It is precisely this type of moral time and effort by human beings that was implemented with Lazarus' burial preparations 2000 years ago that we utilize in ethical funeral service practices and preparations today. The human moral inclinations and intentions as funeral directors/embalmers are essentially the same; only the materials used to implement these moral inclinations and intentions have changed over time.

To complete the examination of the "Religious Convictions as a Guide" criterion, we will review the four Gospel accounts of Jesus' death and burial, focusing on the moral and reverential care that was extended to the body of Jesus by the ones left to tend to this responsibility after His death. It is through the Gospel accounts of the burial of Jesus that we are able to decipher and decode the direct ethical and moral values of reverently caring for the dead which continue to permeate so much of Western civilization. It is the preparation and entombment accounts of Jesus' death that lay much of the foundations of modern practices in caring for our sacred dead.

The Burial of Jesus Christ

Comments

First, in all the Gospel accounts Jesus was laid in a tomb owned by Joseph of Arimathea. The tomb was new and had not been used before. In Matthew, Mark and Luke, Jesus is wrapped carefully in clean linen cloth according to Jewish burial customs and traditions. Mark describes this linen shroud as "fine" and was purchased by Joseph of Arimathea. Matthew and Mark speak of Mary Magdalene and others watching and sitting while the burial took place; whereas, Luke speaks of a group of women from Galilee coming to see the burial. In Mark and Luke the women intend to formally prepare the corpse of Jesus for burial.

All this information corresponds to the living moral of the Ethic of Reverence for the Dead being practiced in scripture, but it is in the book of John that one sees this ethical standard and moral action placed into its full context.

Preparing Christ for Entombment According to Jewish Burial Customs

In the account of Jesus' entombment John writes that about 100 pounds of a special mixture of myrrh and aloes was used in conjunction with strips of linen to bind the corpse of Jesus. This mixture was part of the concoction that was offered to Jesus while He was on the cross to help numb His excruciating pain, which he refused.

Myrrh was not a native plant to Palestine and was very expensive. This type of mixture was used as a method of odor control in ancient Jewish burial practices.

The sacred remains of Jesus were then reverently placed in a new tomb which was located in a garden.

In studying the Gospel of John and the account of how Jesus was cared for after death, one can see many ethical and moral standard and principles that are still practiced and maintained to this day, which reflect the sensitivities of many people concerning the moral practice of the Ethic of Reverence for the Dead.

Jesus was buried in a tomb, and it was a new tomb never used before. Today it is a morally honored standard of action to use a single, unused burial space for a sacred dead person, and our cemeteries most often resemble a garden, which takes many hours of work and moral focus to create and maintain.

Today as a moral standard there is high value placed on the pastoral scenes, the morally sensitive scenes of death as compared in contrast to the brutal mass burials that were witnessed in Nazi Germany during the Second World War. Few people today would view or defend the treatment of the sacred dead as seen in the Nazi concentration camps as being anything other than ethically repugnant and morally bankrupt.

The burial garden concept of flowers and green grass has for millenniums of time served as a human moral reflection of our attempts to help buffer the perceived ugliness and brutality of death. Also soft green grass, beautiful flowers, dew drops and pristine gardens have for time in memoriam been associated with images of the afterlife, or what Heaven must be like.

Jesus was also bound by and dressed in fine white linens. Today it is a moral custom for the living to bring fine clothing for use during a funeral ceremony for a deceased human being. Often, new clothing is morally implemented and used for a burial, and in Orthodox Judaism fine white linen shrouds are still used by the living for burial which reflects the living's time-honored link to ancient moral burial customs.

Horrific images of nude corpses being bulldozed into burial ditches in the Nazi concentration camps (and other political regimes throughout history) and our almost universal moral revulsion of seeing such brutal images remain a poignant moral reminder to humanity of the consequences of what can happen when the Ethic of Reverence for the Dead is ignored, abandoned, or worse, forgotten – its significance not recognized or even spoken about.

As the great Harvard philosopher George Santayana said "A people who forget their history are condemned to repeat it."

Can it be that we are today forgetting the history of the Ethic of Reverence for the Dead? What is our culture's moral barometer today concerning the ethical care of our dead?

The Gospel accounts tell of people being present for the burial of Jesus. Today we still observe this custom by having public funeral services and public committal services at the cemetery and or crematory. Living people participating in death rituals is the visual reality of the Ethic of Reverence for the Dead in action.

Finally, the body of Jesus was anointed and treated with spices, fragrant oils like myrrh and possibly aloe. The fragrant mixture of this oil concoction was almost certainly implemented as a retardant to the formation of natural obnoxious odors, and, hence, was a method of protection from the unpleasantness of decomposition for the living in order for them to make the necessary funerary observances. This was done so the living could more comfortably morally act as participants in the rites, rituals and ceremonies which held moral meaning in their own experience of life. Today the invention of modern chemical preparation of a sacred deceased human being is the same; only the techniques and materials used have changed with technology.

In our treatment of the ethical criterion provided by using religious convictions as a guide, it is safe to assess and conclude that the Judeo-Christian tradition presents an honored, ancient and reverent ethic to morally care for the dead, by action on the part of the living.

A word of caution: in a real sense there are those who work not only to challenge and reject this ethic, but who would work diligently to destroy it by convincing people that taking care of the dead is not such a profound issue. They lead innocent people to conclude that the wise course to follow is to underestimate the moral consequences of abandoning this ethic and hence, do away with it entirely if they could, there, of course they claim, being no moral consequences for the living.

Fortunately, for the present time anyway, the ancient concept of ethical care of the dead by morally acting and caring people still prevails, but this value must be re-articulated and protected constantly, and it is the professional responsibility of the funeral servant to do this.

To conclude this portion of the text we offer a definition of the ethic, Reverence for the Dead.

VI. THE DEFINITION OF THE ETHIC OF REVERENCE FOR THE DEAD

Because it is a clear human truth that the dead cannot take care of themselves nor defend their own dignity, it is essential to determine by continued careful thought and analysis the ends of establishing the absolute standard of ethical principles concerning an answer to the moral question: What is the universal good in a basic care of the dead? The ethical thinking and moral good is this:

That human beings live an intentionally conscious moral standard and inviolate ethical principle which is directed to the human good in realizing that by our own individual moral actions that we are morally enhanced in establishing, requiring and demanding respect and honor to all the helpless sacred dead.

This ethical principle requires both our ethical developed thinking through study and introspection, and our individual moral actions extended to the helpless deceased worldwide who are entrusted into the care of living human beings worldwide.

The Ethic of Reverence for the Dead is the basic moral foundational premise of the funeral service profession. It is through the continued development, articulation, discussion, study and analysis of these ethical standards and moral activities that we are exposed and enlightened to the fundamental validation of contemporary death care, funeral care and preparation and preservation practices.

Through the deliberate and educated preparation of the dead humankind is simply implementing modern technology in order to ethically fulfill our built-in acknowledgement of an ancient emotive instinct to reverently and morally care for the dead; in other words, to morally act on what has happened.

It is the time-honored responsibility of the professional funeral service practitioner to look beyond the surface of contemporary funeral, burial and cremation practices and realize the historic depth of this ethic and to also be alert to the real present-day situation that this ethic in many communities is slipping away and that the care of the dead is morally falling off the conscience of many communities.

Funeral service practitioners are charged with the maintenance of this ethical standard. Maintenance of the Ethic of Reverence for the Dead is of vital importance, for in a very real sense all the subsequent psycho-social values of caring for the dead and funeral, burial and cremation observances find their moral origins of human need discovered in this ethical standard. It is certain that through the habitual practice of the Ethic of Reverence for the Dead, our professional attitudes will be continually maintained and enhanced. But this moral outcome must be diligently worked; it just does not magically happen.

VII. LIVING THE ETHIC OF REVERENCE FOR THE DEAD – THE PSYCHO/SOCIAL IMPACT OF THE ETHIC

The human person is basically a social creature. We talk, write, move, work and play in interaction with others. The processes of social interactions take on all sorts of dimensional aspects. The human person can have shallow or very deep interactions; the human can act with indifference or with profound sympathy and feeling. The human can laugh, shout, whisper, frown, smile and cry. The human person can exhibit these and a thousand more characteristics in the course of just one day of life. Through this complex web of daily interactions we experience life. It is through this remarkable process of interaction that we create attachments and it is from human attachments that not only emotional experiences are created, but springing from our interactions is also the development of ethics. Moral actions and attachments to others go hand in hand. Only human beings can be moral.

Attachments vary from one person to another. Attachments can be deep, shallow, indifferent, joyful, and loyal and yes, painful. When attachments end, usually the result is that someone is left feeling the emotion of grief.

This section of the book will focus on the deep attachment that is created when people enter into a significant relationship. Subsequently, we will examine and explore the results of when death cuts the attachment, and what role the Ethic of Reverence for the Dead plays in moral grief work and its aftermath.

HUMAN ATTACHMENTS

As stated before, attachments can be deep or shallow. Take the simple example of the newspaper delivery boy. A person receives the evening paper day after day, sees the paper boy, sometimes says hello, and then simply goes his or her own way. We are aware and cognizant of the delivery boy, but for an array of reasons we never form a deep sense of attachment to this person. If the paper route is changed, or if the paper boy resigns, this loss would probably not create a deep profound sense of separation, or acute grief. Lives would continue basically unaffected.

Now let us explore and examine the profound attachments of life. This is not like the shallow attachment to the newspaper delivery boy. Within the profound and committed realm of human attachments are the "deep links" - the type of attachments that literally change the course of our lives. Here, our attachments are massive and deep and complicated – they are interwoven psychological bonds that are extremely powerful and when the status of these attachments changes lives change permanently. It is most often in this attachment of complicated interwoven and highly charged emotional atmospheres that our internal securities, satisfactions and devotions are maintained. In this powerful realm of attachment, literally every part of the human psyche is used. Through daily visual and interactive repetition of the deep attachments, our relationships with the significant person or object undergo a type of memory layering process in our brain. The neurons literally create perceptual neurological patterns of recognition and perception. So deep are these profound attachment processes that there are instances in which the individual involved in these intense interactions are actually unaware of the massive dimensions that their attachments have taken until the attachment is terminated by some type of ultimate separation experience like death.

The "how and why" of attachments are baffling. Attachments are embryonic in origin. They flourish throughout life, and they can be so powerful as to continue even beyond the grave through memories. Dimensional aspects of attachments are often unconscious, and because they can be unconscious, individuals are often unaware of how deeply their own behaviors and attitudes are controlled and affected by them. Attachments arise from countless life experiences. They come from suckling the breast, or by seeing a repetitive daily vision of someone or something. They come from a turn of the lip or the arch of an eyebrow. Attachments are created by the sound of a voice, the color of someone's eyes, the color and texture of someone's hair, the style and manner of dress, the person's movements, and the list goes on and on. All these and countless other sights, sounds, sensations and experiences help to form the identification of the core connection of attachments.

It is fortunate, indeed, that humans have the capacity for this type of identification and attachment because our attachment capabilities and capacities often culminate in those very special, deep, cherished and singular relationships with significant people that become one of a series of the great joyful experiences in life.

There is another aspect of attachments, however. For while it is true that from deep relationships we experience the joy of love, it is equally true that from these deep love relationships, these deep attachments, we also experience the inevitable anguish of separation, loss and grief.

The flip side of the coin of love is grief. They simply go hand in hand; one cannot exist without the other. Painful as this might be to accept, what we are about to say is a brutally true fact of human existence: Love does not exist without grief. Taking a risk of loving always involves taking the risk of grieving. In the end, our relationships are not permanent – they too die.

It is through this process of repetitive life experiences with significant others that our attachments are rooted. As the theories of attachments attest, our connecting abilities with other people go very deep. By this process of repetitive attachment, a familiarity with the perceptual characteristics of the significant other is created and is firmly imprinted on our brains. This imprinting is done by the constant repetitive exposure to the loved object and is not to be underestimated or undervalued.

The imprinting process develops a mental picture that is created in our brains and can be referred to as the "body image." The body image to which we are attached is usually reinforced unconsciously and consciously through our own personal interactive experiences with the particular person. The body image is constantly reinforced because for us to be in communication we must relate or respond in one way or another to this created sensory body image picture.

HUMAN SEPARATION

"My mother looks this way and my father looks different from my mother" – that is how simple the body image works in our minds. We then form the habit of relating to, recognizing and identifying our significant others based upon the familiar body image to which our senses have become attached. Because the repetitive exposure to the familiar body images is often intensively reinforced over an extensive period of time, and because our culture is powerfully death denying, innocent people can form an emotional attitude of the unrealistic permanency in the attached relationship. It becomes easy and common for individuals who are profoundly attached to each other to feel confident that the relationship will last forever and that death has nothing to do with them or their attached relationships. As irrational as this may sound, it is nevertheless true and happens constantly. And while we all know consciously that such limitless and physically immortal permanence in even the best, most profound relationship is simply not possible, many live under the meaningless idea that death will not intrude and end the interaction. This though is a lie. Our relationships are not infinite; they are finite and they too must die either through physical separation or physical death.

When people are living under this erroneous idea that death has no place in their life experience, and, hence, they are not motivated to generate any information about death, this condition has a name: it is called **death illiteracy**. When death illiteracy is present the Ethic of Reverence for the Dead collapses. Death illiteracy is epidemic in the American culture. Based on the definition of our ethic, this state of affairs is immoral and many innocent people are affected unwittingly by this cultural situation.

For example, the American educational system spends hours, months, and years teaching reading, writing and mathematics, and even sex education. It is the moral thing to do to educate our children – hardly anyone disagrees with that ethical standard.

We even teach children in kindergarten facts and truth about the beginnings of life, how life is created. However, the culture unfortunately educates our children on nothing concerning the end of life. The Ethic of Reverence for the Dead morally calls out for recognition and equal time, for death illiteracy is taking a tremendous toll on how people view living life. Possessing and embracing a morally mature attitude towards the reality of death in order to improve the quality of life by knowing what a mature attitude towards death encompasses (that death is universal, inevitable, and irreversible) is a rare, personal characteristic in our contemporary culture. This happens, but it is rare.

It is important that the funeral service practitioner understands and appreciates the complex processes of attachments and separations, for it is from the psychological process of attachments that the Ethic of Reverence for the Dead is necessary and the subsequent moral needs for death rites, rituals and ceremonies arise. Without human attachments there would morally be little, if any, need for rites, rituals and ceremonies and also little need for the definition and analysis and articulation of the ethic. A death ritual which reflects the Ethic of Reverence for the Dead is always based on human attachments to the deceased. In its most elementary form, death rituals are a social function which reflects the truth of the human capacity for deep attachments and the expression of high moral actions and behaviors.

Even in the instance of indigent, unknown, and forgotten dead human beings, the Ethic of  Reverence for the Dead requires the living to give moral attention to the reverential care of these unfortunate sacred dead human beings. In fact in the legal system the Ethic of Reverence for the Dead is very much alive and seen when municipalities, county governments, and sometimes even the church or temple intervene morally to insure that even the least of these receive reverential care when death occurs.

THE INDIGENT BURIAL AND THE ETHIC OF REVERENCE FOR THE DEAD

Death, in the end, always brings a finality which challenges most of the coping resources of the psyche. With death comes the final realization that what was once thought to be permanent and everlasting is in truth physically temporary and truly finite. The death rate is a pure 100%; no one escapes this planet alive. With the mental realization of the finality of death comes the long and often painful emotion and process of grief and mourning. It is during this mourning process - this special allotted time that the bereaved are challenged to divest themselves of their close attachments to the dead person and are asked to begin and hopefully eventually reinvest in other people and reinvent new life experiences. The process of mourning is vital and necessary for healthy grieving. This importance springs from the awareness and respect people have concerning the Ethic of Reverence for the Dead by not morally underestimating its significance to them.

There was a time in the history of death care when the Ethic of Reverence for the Dead was a strong presence in living life and in this period death rituals and mourning periods lasted for days; it was a living present moral force. In our present culture of death-denial, death rituals are now routinely abbreviated and reduced to hours. Critical mourning periods are often today seen as ancient customs from an old-fashioned past and worse people who continue to observe these wise moral activities are viewed as odd, strange, and out of touch – not "cool".

However, Orthodox Jews still morally and religiously observe the sitting of Shiva, observing the Sholoshim and the Year of Mourning. This type of moral mourning activity begs for attention and exploration. In Orthodox Judaism ethical funeral and burial practices are full of ancient moral wisdom. For example, in Orthodox Judaism the Chevra Kadisha - "The Holy Burial Society" - is a group of Jewish men and women who morally see to it that the sacred bodies of deceased Jews are prepared for burial according to Jewish traditions and are literally and morally protected from immoral desecration, willful or not, until burial. Also many Jewish bereaved have the presence of the "Shomer" which is a Hebrew word for "guard". The Shomer sits with the deceased until the time of the funeral and recites Psalms and prayers for the deceased and may also study Torah on the family's behalf. The Orthodox Jewish moral action approach to living the Ethic of Reverence for the Dead is clearly the exception to the contemporary standard of mourning behavior in the American culture which is roughly this: bury or burn your loved one on Wednesday, and be back to work on Thursday.

In this climate of the rampant abbreviated death rituals and ridiculously abbreviated mourning periods, the Ethic of Reverence of the Dead gets hidden under a basket of silence, avoidance and anxieties, and many life-wisdom lessons, which can indeed improve a person's moral approach to life, are lost. This state of affairs is indeed unfortunate.

VIII. THE ETHICAL CONUNDRUM

It is often heard in conversation that it is better to remember the dead as they were when they were alive, hence avoiding looking at the dead body. This type of thinking represents the ultimate in death-denial, and hence is also disconnected with the ethical standard of revering the dead.

Part of the definition of healthy psychology is honest confrontation with the reality of life events. Let us analyze the reality of death in reference to our ethical position.

Here is the brutally honest fact: the deceased is NOT ALIVE; he or she is dead! Hence the comment, "I would rather remember them alive," is a form of death denial and a simple contradiction in ethical terms. Ethical behavior first and foremost requires truth and honesty, and the honest confrontation of the reality of death is necessary and a very valuable step for the mourners to take. Seeing the deceased person or a symbol of the deceased person, (in cases where it is impossible to view the dead body) which represents the reality of death has been endorsed by thanatologists since the subject first was studied academically in the late 1950s.

The idea is simple - seeing is believing. By seeing and touching the deceased or a symbol of the deceased that is familiar to the bereaved, the mourners have the necessary visual and physical opportunity which is needed to verify the reality and honest truth of the reality of the death. In cases where the deceased is lost forever, where there is not a chance for the bereaved to establish the reality of death, risks for complicated bereavement exist. In this instance, secondary symbols, representing a remembered body image of the sacred decedent can be helpful (i.e. photographs, personal mementos) but they are still secondary – the actual sacred body of the decedent is always the preference in the Ethic of Reverence for the Dead.

It is very common in the study of grief to observe bereaved persons denying the death of someone to whom attachments were profound. The process of denial takes many forms. It is customarily observed in an avoidance of contact with the reality of death – namely the dead person, the corpse, the cadaver.

At first glance this avoidance may appear to reflect the attitude that the bereaved person has his or her emotional act together. Adding to this is the fact that the bereaved are often rewarded by others in the culture for this type of rationality; it is seen as "cool", and people quickly indict viewing the dead body as "barbaric" and "pagan".

The case of bereavement and ethical care of the dead is not so simple as to be handled by this type of rational logical thought only. The very clinical definition of grief is that it is the emotion of loss – it is not rational, it is not sterile, it is not logical, it is **emotional**. It is important that everyone involved with bereavement care recognize this attitude for what it truly is – the denial of death and a moral unawareness of the significance of the Ethic of Reverence for the Dead.

The case of human separation and grief can never fully be brushed away through mental and rhetorical rationalizations or minimizing honest ethical behavior and action in confronting the dead. Often in bereavement the people who are the most grieved by the death are the same people who most need to establish the reality of death, but are precisely the people who opt to take the road of least resistance and avoid any visual and tactile confrontation with the actual dead body image. Also many well-intended people are unwitting conspirators in supporting and endorsing such avoidance decisions and behaviors. Establishing the reality of death is always an issue of need more than want. Clearly most people do not want to see their loved ones dead, but in fact they need to see the truth and reality of this highly significant event in their life.

In exploring this concept of visually seeing the dead and being in actual contact with the dead, a brief examination of the use of the funeral effigy will be helpful in giving a further example of the moral actions of people in times long ago implementing the Ethic of Reverence for the Dead.

Many times in life the meaning of a word is lost. The word "effigy" is an example of this. Today when effigies are used they are hung or burned expressing protest and annoyance. This use of an effigy for expressing political or social disapproval has been common enough for all of us to know what it means.

However, in reference to our topic of the Ethic of Reverence for the Dead, and confronting death visually and tactilely, the subject of the effigy is essentially a much larger and important concept than an angry crowd burning something which resembles a person who has caused angst or disappointments.

There is another and more important use of the effigy. This more positive use has been employed for centuries in rites, rituals and ceremonies, in funerary practices, but has almost completely disappeared in the last century.

In times long past kings and queens had elaborate and lifelike effigies created by artists to be used exclusively at their funeral rites. They had this effigy completed long before they were dead. Not only were the funeral effigies an acknowledgement of the ethical reverential funeral care of the particular royal prior to their actual death, effigies also had a political purpose. The social and political protection of the people of the kingdom was bound up in the life of the royal king or queen or both. When any royal regent died there was always a risk of political unrest and a struggle for power. Because of this real threat it was of great importance to the royal dynasty that there would be an orderly and ceremonially significant event to affirm, confirm and verify that the royal was indeed actually dead and to make the transfer of power – and this ceremony was the royal funeral.

Communication was limited during this time and the notification of the death of a royal traveled slowly through the kingdom. Travel was slow and it took weeks and sometimes months for the princes, political officials and the general populace to gather for the extensive royal funeral events. Quite obviously, if there was a delay of two weeks or more between the time of the royal death and the time of the royal funeral events, the dead body of the royal would be offensive and hence in no condition to be used.

It was at these royal funeral events that the carefully prepared effigy was brought out to play an important role in the funeral ceremony; it reflected the royal body image, the symbol of death, and the reality of the royal's death because people could visually see the funeral effigy and this was proof positive that the royal was indeed dead.

When the actual royal body was buried under the floor of some famous church or cathedral, the symbolic royal sarcophagus remained in view with the remembered effigy of the royal on top clearly in sight. This effigy remained highly significant as the focal point for the communities acting out of their grief for years to come. This is a premier example of people hundreds of years ago morally by their actions implementing the Ethic of Reverence for the Dead.

However, this connection between our modern day and the past has yet another story concerning the effigy concept and the Ethic of Reverence for the Dead.

In time some of the other dignitaries in the kingdom, but non royals, decided that they too were entitled to buy their own effigy. Thus developed this special form of art and craft that made the reclining statues, the body image effigies of people, available to more than royalty and which were ultimately used at funerals and as memorials after death. One of the world's finest examples of the body image "effigy" is the collection which can be seen at Westminster Abbey in London. Westminster Abbey offers the visitor a wonderful moral example of the Ethic of Reverence for the Dead in action.

The down side to this was that effigies (making wooden body images) were expensive. Those who could not afford a sculptured effigy later used a personal death mask as a full body image substitute as effigies tended to be. The death mask was designed to give a likeness to the person. Museums throughout the world still show these partial effigies and death masks (the body image) of famous people.

About the middle of the last century the use of effigies and death masks gradually faded out and now these practices are practically unknown. The reason, of course, is that society developed a better way of providing the mourners with a body image likeness or effigy that they could use as a focal point during death rituals, while at the same time expressing the Ethic of Reverence for the Dead.

Today the effigy and death masks are things of the past, but the need to remember the dead human being is still a motivator and hence the culture embraced a new method of establishing the identity of the dead person. That body image today is the restored and preserved sacred dead body, which now can be easily maintained for days and weeks in order for the practical (transportation of the sacred dead) ethical, religious, psychological purposes of death rites, rituals, and ceremonies to take place.

Put simply, the modern practice of employing restorative art and chemical preparation of a dead human body provides the best possible contemporary effigy or even a death mask at the least possible cost. What only kings and members of the royalty could afford a few centuries ago is now available to every member of the community.

A thousand years ago myrrh and spices was used to create a lasting body image, five hundred years ago the wooden effigy and the death mask were used, today it is sophisticated chemical preparation, but regardless of the materials and techniques used, the moral and ethical intent to create a remembered body image to aid the mourners in their bereavement experience is precisely the same.

Psychological research has established that the moment of truth, the moments to hold onto in the individual death experience, comes when the living confronts the dead body of the one they mourn. This may be the most significant, single therapeutic and ethical event in the death experience process. The obligation to face reality, the chance to express valid feelings and the privilege of group support and the actions and consequences of ethical behaviors are all made possible through modern restoration and preservation methods.

In a death-denying, death-defying culture as we certainly live in, the value of this ethic, and of this moment to hold in truth and honesty as to what has really happened becomes of even greater importance for it can well save the mourners from innocently and out of death illiteracy rejecting the significance of this event which can lead to serious personality change and physical illness.

People who have access to saying good bye and farewell to the ultimate symbol of the death event, namely the prepared and preserved dead body, are fortunate.

IX. THE PSYCHOLOGY OF THE ETHIC OF REVERENCE FOR THE DEAD

Dr. Erich Lindemann was one of the great pioneers in the study of grief management. Dr. Lindemann took the position that there is really no escaping the slow wisdom of grief. This act is part of the before mentioned courage and honesty aspect that is discovered in the Ethic of Reverence for the Dead. Dr. Lindemann took the position that avoidance of the dead body is always done at the psychological peril of the bereaved and that avoiding the body image at first seems convenient in the immediate phase of acute grief.

But in truth, Dr. Lindemann says, this type of death "convenience" is an illusion. In time the necessity to view the body image becomes a major issue in post bereavement. Dr. Lindemann maintained that a common trait in persons experiencing complicated bereavement is that they are unable to

recall a clear mental picture of the body image of their lost loved one in the state of physical death. According to Dr. Lindemann establishing a clear mental image of the deceased person to whom attachments have been made is an important ingredient in creating a wise basis for all subsequent grief activities. A cloudy image of the deceased person or no image at all creates a dishonest mental appraisal of the realities of the truth of the death environment and of what has in reality and truth undeniably happened.

Dr. Erich Lindemann 1900 - 2005

Dr. Lindemann believed that the most significant benefit of funeral rites, rituals and ceremonies happens at the moment when the truth about the reality of death, the utter unblemished truth, occurs within the bereaved person's mind. It is at this moment of truth, this establishment of the reality of death by actually seeing and touching the dead that serves as the psychological framework for the human validation of preparation and preservation of the dead, and it is a clear expression in tough honest action of living the Ethic of Reverence for the Dead. This author concludes that the actual viewing and touching of a dead human body is the best way to break through death-denial thoughts harbored by a bereaved person, and in so doing, to take full advantage of the wisdom held within the thinking of the ethic.

Many believe, as the Rev. Dr. Edgar N. Jackson did, that the preparation, preservation and beautification of the dead is to make the dead body "presentable" for viewing, much like in life how that person would have to prepare for meeting others by washing, combing, etc., before greeting people in public, (naturally in death the dead body is unable to do this for themselves and our ethic calls out for someone to do this for them). The concepts of Reverence for the Dead, decent disposition and dignity in death, all culminate in the attitude that the dead body somehow be prepared for viewing so as not to be offensive during the process of rites, rituals and ceremonies.

Rev. Dr. Edgar N. Jackson
1910 – 1994

One of the hallmarks in a career and a calling to be involved professionally in funeral service is the bedrock of ethical thinking that just because you are dead does not mean you are not still a human being. Live human beings prize dignity, honor and respect. Since the dead cannot defend these ethical standards for themselves, the contemporary funeral professional is morally charged with this high duty and responsibility to do it for them (or some other group such as the Jewish Chevra Kadisha).

The motto of the old Canadian College of Mortuary Arts and Sciences at the University of Toronto Banting Institute summed up this ethical principle very well: "Sic Vos Non Solum Vobis" which translates to: "With Us They Are Not Alone."

In addition, the famous grief thinker Dr. Geoffrey Gorer suggested that people act out their grief.

Acting out death rituals in a visual manner, with the body present (the ultimate ethical symbol of death) offers stability, security, social control and tradition in a time of chaos, confusion, anxiety and remorse.

Because ritualized death activities take time, educated preparation and preservation procedures of the dead furnishes the family, community and friends the necessary and very important time to organize and implement their specific death rituals.

It can be said that a funeral service is an ethical psycho-drama whereby the family, friends and community of the deceased are the protagonists in a life play which dramatizes the fact that a life has been lived. The dead body image, properly prepared, offers the living important time which is necessary for the implementation of rites, rituals and ceremonies on the community level, and for introspection and discernment at the individual personal level. The prepared and preserved body image aids in a person's reflections upon the ethical respect held between people in a given community.

The prepared and preserved body image permits temporarily an open, realistic acceptance of death. In this type of honest confrontation there is no opportunity to escape from the truth of the reality of death which in itself is unethical because pure objective ethics always requires confronting the truth first and foremost no matter how painful it might be.

The prepared and preserved body image truthfully confronts the denial of death and helps to provide an atmosphere of emotional stability in a safe place where high emotional states and expressions of grief and loss are not only accepted, but are understood.

By confronting the numerous frightening and lonely feelings caused by the emotional conflicts of death denial, the prepared and preserved body image helps to act as a catharsis for emotional states such as panic, fear, frustration and guilt. Visual contact with the prepared and preserved body image aids in establishing necessary and healthy modifications of emotional and physical attachments to the deceased. This is ethical mental health, and in a strange way, this is too personal to be private. This may well be why at a funeral everyone is usually invited, but usually no invitations are sent.

Here is how the psychology of the Ethic of Reverence for the Dead works in real life.

Viewing the dead body provides the bereaved with the ethical truth and ethical reality that a death has actually happened. The first viewing tells the bereaved that the death is irreversible.

It is through this first awareness of the truth and reality of physical separation from the dead that leads to the finality of death.

Without this raw ethical truth and reality, the journey of grief will be hindered due to the bereaved working with pure and simple dishonest and incomplete death information. The dead body image morally aids the bereaved almost immediately in action by giving them the honesty of the situation in which death has placed them and which no words can replace. Anything less than honest confrontation with the remembered dead body image is always less than what has actually happened, and the bereaved are working with faulty, unrealistic information, and this is immoral for everyone involved.

With morally truthful and realistic information, and only this type of high principled moral information, can the bereaved with ethical truth and an honest moral experience start to move forward through the process of mourning. This then is the moral authority which is found in the wisdom of embracing the Ethic of Reverence for the Dead.

Two conclusions can now be drawn from the forgoing analysis. First, the properly prepared and recognizable body image is both ethically wise and reflects moral and psychological truth. Second, it is the technical work of the contemporary embalmer which sets the foundation for the moral, truthful reality of death to essentially, tastefully and practically take place.

X. THE ETHIC OF REVERENCE FOR THE DEAD AND DEATH RITES, RITUALS AND CEREMONIES

The human person, as has been mentioned before, is a social creature and we are also ethical creatures. In fact, only human beings can behave ethically or unethically. It is through our ethics and sociality that we locate our maturity and a sense of personal identification. The process of sociality and ethics also leads us to our eventual integrity, integration and our development of continued self-realized ethical standards over a lifetime.

Being ethical is a worthy ideal that people have hoped and endeavored to attain for centuries. Core to our ethical development is our realization that in order to live an effective and balanced life one needs to be social and ethical.

Nowhere does one see this basic need for sociality more clearly than in the ritualistic ethical behavior exhibited by people in what are called "rites of passages".

The human being, in essence, is ritualistic. In fact, it is precisely the purpose of this portion of the text to lead the reader to the conclusion that ritualistic behavior (and particularly the death rituals) is ethically indigenous to the human experience. So entrenched is the makeup of the human being in ritualistic behavior that a failure or corruption of rituals often results in human cataclysm and is an example many times of the failure of our ethical systems.

The thinking that encompasses this part of the text is based in large measure on the collaborative ideas and combined theories of Auguste Comte, Carl. G. Jung, Eric Erickson, and Rudolph Otto. Centered and blended in large measure on the theories and philosophies of the these giants in human intellectual thought an analysis will be made of their theories in relationship to rituals which link ethics, psychology, sociology, anthropology and theology to the values of emotional experiences gained through the death rituals.

Before entering into the analysis of Jung, Erickson and Otto, it will be helpful to briefly examine the development of psychological attitudes towards the values of rituals in general and the expansion of the holistic and ethical definition of the human being in particular. We start with Auguste Comte.

In the early days in the development of psychology, much resentment existed because primitive psychology was constantly guilty of the crime of reductionism. That is, primitive psychology tried to reduce the human to chemical equations, predictable behaviors and the like. Even today this tendency is seen in many psychological schools of thought.

Auguste Comte 1798 – 1857

One of the pioneers in the "reductionist" school of psychology was Auguste Comte. The founder of a school of psychology called "French Positivism," he was one of the early reductionists in psychological studies. Comte maintained that if one could not measure or experience something with the senses, then that "something" was not worth studying.

According to Comte people were nothing more than chemical reactions. Comte maintained that while a person may be tall, handsome, beautiful and intelligent, these characteristics were simply a result of chemicals reacting together. He represented a school of thinking that reduced the human being to purely a biological event in nature. Not surprisingly the ethical approach of Comte was that life was a series of brutal and senseless happenings which in the end could be accurately defined as being absurd. The Ethic of Reverence for the Dead was absent from Comte's thinking.

As the Comte reductionist controversy continued, the theories of a Viennese physician named Dr. Sigmund Freud (1856 – 1939) were being developed. Freud's conclusions concerning the nature of the human person startled his contemporaries, and even to this day the mention of Freud's name sparks reactions in many people.

As controversial as Freud's theories may be for some, he nonetheless was one of the first thinkers to see the human experience as a complex web of internal struggles and not simply chemical reactions. To Dr. Freud these human struggles were made up of memories and insecurities most of which were located in a hidden part of the mind that could not be seen, but which exerted tremendous control and influence over one's life. Dr. Freud was moving in the direction of defining the human as being more than a bunch of chemicals working together.

This brief sketch allows the reader to see the slow movement that thought concerning the psychology of the human person has taken over the years. For centuries many religions acknowledged only the spiritual and depraved nature of humankind. With the advent of psychology, the mental processes of the mind were acknowledged as being equal with the spiritual and today great emphasis on the physical well-being of the human body is being emphasized.

This developed holistic definition of the human has, at its root, the essential ethical and ritualistic behaviors of people as being a vital component for one's general well-being and the integration of mind, body and spirit. The Ethic of Reverence for the Dead is holistic in its pure essence, because the death rate is 100% and grief is grief and pain is pain worldwide. This ethic by its very nature embraces the entire mind, body and spirit of both the dead and the living.

Not surprisingly however, both Comte and Freud de-emphasized and rationalized rituals, saying that rituals only reflected basic human insecurities, and in the end rituals and ethics were favorable to contributing to the safe order of society, but that was it. In the end ethics and rituals were nothing more than methods of social control and social order.

It took the thinking of one of Freud's greatest students, Dr. Carl G. Jung, to re-define, re-integrate and re-introduce the absolute ethical value and absolute necessity of ritualistic participation in one's life, community and world as part of our journey to mature self-realization. Dr. Jung maintained that life was much more than a mere biological event. There were other forces, other notions, and other super-natural occurrences in life, which were observable to everyone and which exerted a tremendous influence on existence.

Of these influences Dr. Jung maintained that ethics and rituals were two of the most significant.

Dr. Carl G. Jung, a Neo-Freudian, and in his own right a pioneer in human psychology, gave us theories of the human personality that are very valuable in forming an appreciation of the social and psychological values which are linked specifically to the processes of the death rituals and the Ethic of Reverence for the Dead.

Dr. Jung saw the psychological life as a universal phenomenon whereby identification with what he termed the "collective unconscious" linked all humanity together.

This mental and ethical condition and unity is what Dr. Jung means by the term "collective unconscious." Given the wide diversities of the human person, the idea of a collective unconscious may at first be confusing. Clarification can be found if we realize that while we differ from others in much of · our identity, there are certain symbols, that Dr. Jung calls archetypes, that link us all together in the vast collective unconscious. Archetypes are primordial symbols common to all human kind.

Dr. Carl G. Jung 1875 – 1961

For example, in all cultures the dead body symbolizes the reality of death and in all cultures the funeral ritual is an absolute universal, and the Ethic of Reverence for the Dead has an absolute history and presence.

The collective unconscious is a mental unifying agent. The idea of the collective unconscious says that we may differ in regional, racial and religious attitudes, but there exist constants and unifications in our mental and ethical makeup with which everyone can eventually identify and understand.

Another way to state this is that all humanity has these common symbols that everyone globally understands and associates with since the beginning of existence. A wonderful example of this would be that since our existence began the death rate has been a perfect, even 100%. This honest fact was true in the world of the Neanderthal and they used the corpse as the common symbol of death. Dead people are universally common symbols of death.

Funeral rituals, with the symbol of death (the dead body) being present, would be an excellent example of a universal ethical predisposition and pattern that is common to all people worldwide. The collective unconscious is then a type of mass identification which unifies people through common predispositions and patterns of ethical behavior that can be learned and passed on.

It is interesting to note that Dr. Jung saw religious convictions, another universal common pattern in all cultures, emerge out of the deep-seated collective unconscious.

Dr. Jung thought religious convictions originated out of the collective unconscious as a result of our confrontation with the world around us. Here it is important to see the connection between his idea of the collective unconscious, and the subsequent tendency to ritualize death in a religious and ethical manner. This is what is meant when we speak of the Ethic of Reverence for the Dead being built into our very being. This built-in capacity is reflected in and through the archetypes of the collective unconscious. The funeral is one of the oldest cultural universals which are common to all humanity.

The idea of the collective unconscious linking all humanity is supported when one recognizes that the funeral is a primary example of a cultural universal. The funeral, reverential care of the dead, and the dead themselves, all become and are collective unconscious archetypes.

Dr. Jung identified birth, re-birth, death, power, magic, unity, the hero, the child, God, demons, the wise old man, mother earth, and animals as basic archetypes of the collective unconscious (deepest unconscious mind, genetically inherited and common to all human beings). Hence, while our identities may differ worldwide there are archetypal images that link us together in a common humanity. The funeral ritual, common to all cultures, is an excellent example of this phenomenon, and the practice, of the Ethic of Reverence for the Dead propels the ritual to accomplish what it has been designed to do throughout history and even before history was recorded. This ethic is simple because of its historical purity and authenticity.

Research has shown that frequently grieving individuals who do not view the dead body have frightening dreams about the deceased. Individuals who ignore the ethical lessons had in revering the dead and hence who do not confront the realities of death by viewing the dead encounter dream states which actually support the denial of death. In other words, the grieving person actually makes the dead person come alive in dream states. Dream encounters in which a messenger comes to the door and announces that the deceased person is not really dead are common. People wake from these dreams confused and require additional time to once again readjust during waking time to the realities of death, of course until they have another dream.

Conversely, people who do view the archetype of death, in other words, the dead human body, have no such dream states. Their dreams appear not to be painful, but instead are pleasant recollections of the past. The deceased person is known to be dead, and the psyche of the bereaved accepts this difficult truth. This acceptance is supported by ethical truth of the reality of death.

One of the interesting facts of Jungian psychology is that Dr. Jung was able to overcome an excessive individualization of the psyche. Being a person who is addicted to individualism (me, myself and I approach to life) makes moral standards of life very difficult if not almost impossible to accomplish. The Ethic of Reverence for the Dead first and foremost in life is a sharing moral position with other people and this type of sharing action is best witnessed in the ritual activities such as at wakes, visitations, calling hours, memorial services, lunches, webinar ceremonies, internet death rituals and today a myriad of other death and funeral rituals.

Dr. Jung maintained that healing and growth, which means facing the harsh realities of life, were best and most effectively dealt with through ethically honest relationships and ethically wise and sound rituals.

Growth without relationships is an illusion and ritual participation assists in this growth process. Dr. Jung did not dismiss religious expression in the quest for individual mental health, as Dr. Freud did in the early part of his career.

Dr. Jung maintained that within the religious journey there could be found countless archetypal images, with death being one powerful example. The Ethic of Reverence for the Dead has at its core the moral position that while the rituals of death take on a myriad of rites, rituals and ceremonies the religious archetypal images that Dr. Jung identifies make ritual participation one of the wisest, most economical and accessible methods of dealing and coping with grief caused by the death of someone we are attached to.

Another thought concerning religious expression and living the Ethic of Reverence for the Dead: religious thought acknowledges first and foremost globally that life is more than a simple random biological event.

Our own bodies and subsequent identities were and are contingent upon the products of our relationships. In the case of the death experience this type of relational growth, this type of social support and interaction is accomplished through the ethical values and social processes of the funeral ritual by practicing the Ethic of Reverence for the Dead.

XI. THE ETHIC OF REVERENCE FOR THE DEAD AND LARGER-THAN-LIFE EXPERIENCES – THE NUMINOUS

Let us now move on to the concept of Rudolph Otto's "numinous" experience in reference to the dead body being present and viewed in the funeral ritual and its moral relevance to the Ethic of Reverence for the Dead.

Rudolph Otto wrote a masterful book called "*The Idea of the Holy*" and in this book he coins the word "numinous." Otto describes the numinous as the "larger-than-life experiences" in life. We will use "larger-than-life" to refer to the numinous through this portion of the text. Otto's approach and thinking is very much related to the work of William James, who we explored in the first section of this book.

Rudolf Otto 1869 - 1937

According to Otto larger-than-life experiences are characterized by feelings of attraction and fear simultaneously toward the same object; a type of psychological paradox. This type of experience is rare; they are definitely NOT ordinary reality, but are actually finite reality which means the experience takes the human being to the outer limits of psychological and religious comfort. Numinous experiences have one thing in common: they are never enjoyable.

An example of the "numinous" experience might be seeing Niagara Falls for the first time and being frightened and terrified at the power of the water, but oddly being simultaneously attracted to

Niagara's utter majesty, beauty and splendor, but feeling great relief when the tour boat turns around and takes you to safety. Another examples of the "numinous" might be seeing the Grand Canyon for the first time and having great attraction to it, but feeling great fear about the possibility of your falling to you death. Another example is read in Genesis when Moses experienced and was confronted by the Burning Bush. Moses is spellbound and utterly terrified at the same moment and the experience altered Moses for the rest of his life.

The numinous experience has another common denominator: the experience changes life forever, nothing is ever the same again – absolutely nothing. The numinous can easily be described as the larger-than-life experience, and most every human being has had something akin to this in their life experiences.

numinous

(adj.) having the power to invoke fear and trembling, yet create fascination and attraction; transcendent; suggesting the presence of divinity

Often times the "numinous" is felt when people fall in love; the people are overjoyed and frightened at the same time, and, as many can attest if the relationship is made legal and permanent, life is changed forever, for good or for bad.

Otto's account of numinous experience identifies two distinct themes: a *mysterium tremendum* (a tremendous mystery) a sense of mystery which evokes fear and trembling; and *mysterium fascinans* (a fascinating mystery) which fascinates and attracts. Viewing a sacred decedent possess both of these experiences.

All religious experiences possess elements of the numinous to some degree and most certainly the Ethic of Reverence for the Dead possess deep elements with what is called the numinous or larger-than-life experience. People effectively relate to these larger-than-life experiences, to the numinous, through rituals and symbols. In fact when words fail, as they often do, in trying to embrace the numinous within the Ethic of Reverence for the Dead, people are motivated to turn to rituals and ceremonies.

The sheer vastness and awesomeness of the typical numinous experience usually makes simple language inadequate to describe the experience. Instead of language, symbols are used through rituals to help comprehend the ultimate unexplainable nature of the numinous, larger-than-life experience

It is clear from the length of this book that describing the Ethic of Reverence for the Dead is also limited by language, words and mere vocabulary. In this way experiencing the reality of death, or another way to say it - the numinous of death, the value and meaning of funeral rituals is something that calls out for experience and participation rather than mere intellectual conversations and words.

The numinous experience and symbols go hand in hand to help us understand the larger-than-life experience. For instance when the Native and First Americans first encountered the Grand Canyon they immediately created gods, symbols and rituals to help them assimilate the literal vastness of this natural wonder. The Grand Canyon is, if it is nothing else, a larger-than-life experience.

For our purposes in this section of the book the following definition of symbols will be used:

"A symbol is a thing which is beside the thing that we see that leads to knowledge other than itself. This deeper notion of symbols helps people make an unknown reality known.

WORLD RELIGIOUS SYMBOLS

Symbols have been used in dealing with the mystery of the numinous experience for centuries by using a visual symbolic substitute that teaches a person lessons about the deeper meaning which is behind the symbol we are looking at.

For instance, the Chalice used in the Mass is not the Eucharist by itself but is a symbol or a substitute for the larger-than-life experience which represents the numinous experience of embracing the Body and Blood of Christ. The Star of David is not the actual larger-than-life religious experience embraced in Judaism, but it is the substitute symbol which people use to connect to that particular Jewish numinous experience.

People always relate in a fuller manner to the numinous experiences of life through rituals. Common, ordinary language and expressions will not accomplish the task of describing the numinous.

Rituals offer us more - when words fail to embrace the numinous experience, people turn to rites, rituals and ceremonies.

Likewise in further defining the Ethic of Reverence for The Dead we too must identify a larger-than-life symbol. In the instance of defining this ethic the dead human body is the ultimate earthly symbol of death, it represents the numinous experience, the larger-than-life experience that is held within the mystery of physical death. The dead body in this ethical framework is the visible substitute for the thing that has really happened – the physical death of a human being who lived life on earth.

The Ethic of Reverence for the Dead is too large a subject matter to take in all at once, so we use a substitute symbol to help and aid us in assimilating the meaning of what revering the dead actually means, we use the archetype of death, specifically the dead body as a substitute buffer, as a ritual cushion to help the survivors assimilate the larger-than-life realities of the death.

Using our definition of symbols it can be assessed that as difficult as it can be in the actions of looking at dead human remains, it is still compelling that no other symbol besides the actual dead human body can lead the bereaved and affected community of mourners to knowledge other than itself (the dead human body).

This "other" kind of knowledge is often times rejected and rationalized by the effected mourners for the very reason that most of life's greatest and most insightful experiences of true knowledge are in essence difficult. As we will see later, it is easy to reject the notion of there being any value in actually viewing the dead, but unfortunately this is also often a cardinal signal that the bereaved do not want to face up to the raw numinous which the body of a loved one can easily create.

However, for all the rationalization, logic and well-intended people who are unwitting conspirators in stopping the numinous of death in its tracks simply because the experience is so humbling, so intimidating and so unpleasant, the fact remains that looking hard and long at the corpse of a human being complies very well with our definition of symbols – "a symbol is a thing which is beside the thing that we see that leads to knowledge other than itself."

The natural question could easily be asked: "What knowledge? We know they are dead." The ultimate symbol of death, which is the dead human body, possesses much knowledge behind the symbol we are looking at. The experience of actually seeing and yes even touching a dead human body motivates and inspires the participants in this valuable activity to think about life, to think about what life means, to ponder relationships past and present, and to reflect on our own behaviors concerning how we treat people, what are our value systems and how can we become better people. Looking at a dead human body, if given time and support, can accomplish this and much more.

We have established that the dead human body is an example of an archetypal numinous. Remember, the numinous fills people with awe and wonder, it makes people fearful yet fascinated at the same time. It is most often a tremendous spiritual experience where people report feeling they are in the presence of divinity. This is precisely what many people report feeling when they view a dead human body.

In the end it is the depth of the numinous experience that makes viewing a dead human being for so many people so difficult, and for this simple reason. When a human being stares into the face of a dead human being they are staring into the reality of their own future. They are staring into the face of their own mortality, and this experience, given the death-denying society that we live in, is unsettling; and given it are very easy to reject viewing a dead person, people make this decision all the time. Sadly the numinous, with all its free and accessible life knowledge is lurking right behind the symbol of death (the dead human body), but in our contemporary society this once-in-a-lifetime experience is often tossed away with a simple wave of a hand, and once it is gone, it is gone forever.

This concept can be stated another way. In the Ethic of Reverence for the Dead, in this unquestionable larger-than-life reality, people utilize the ultimate symbol of death, the dead body (which is a universal archetype) within a moral ritualistic structure (death rites, rituals and ceremonies) to help people better morally understand, assimilate and articulate the larger-than-life event created by death (the numinous). This is one of the essentials contained in the Ethic of Reverence for the Dead.

If one examines the symbolism of global death rituals, many of Dr. Jung's archetypes surface. Think of the following examples: archetype water – used in blessing the body and the grave in many religious traditions; archetype smoke – used in incense burning and other religious rites worldwide; archetype rebirth – used in many theologies and funeral orations to offer hope to the living; archetype unity – used in the sociality of those attending public funerals, Shiva's, Trisagion rituals (Eastern Orthodox) ; archetype God – used in most afterlife concepts; and finally the archetype death – used in the universal human bereavement experience via the dead human body, the ultimate archetypal symbol of death.

We now can see that ethically and symbolically it is no more unusual for a corpse to be used during a funeral ritual than it is for water to be used at a baptism; they are both numinous substitutes which teach the living valuable lessons about the meaning of our larger-than-life experiences. In this ethical system the corpse and water in ritual systems take on the same role in understanding the numinous.

XII. THE ETHIC OF REVERENCE FOR THE DEAD AND THE MORAL NECESSITY OF RITES, RITUALS AND CEREMONIES AS AN IMPORTANT INGREDIENT FOR MENTAL HEALTH

We will next examine ritualistic development in people and how this development reflects the inner core of the collective unconscious, and the numinous as a further expression of the Ethic of Reverence for the Dead. The theories of Dr. Eric Erickson are appropriate for this part of our study. Dr. Erickson's thoughts are based on a continuation of Jungian psychology.

Dr. Erickson maintained that there needs to be a balance of ethical growth between both the chronology and psychology in a person for healthy maturation. In reference to a person's ethical ritualistic development this seems very valid. For example: a small child, without being taught by any adult, will instinctively bury a dead pet upon death.

Erickson calls this built-in tendency for ethical ritualistic behavior the "Ontogeny of Ritualization." The word ontogeny refers to something that is rooted in the biological development of the person; it does not need to be taught.

Clearly this is very close to Jung's concept of the collective unconscious and Neanderthal's primal emotive instinct. Erickson recognizes that rituals are endemic to the formation of a healthy psyche and equally the formation of ethical behavior and that this formation is so vital in our shared human experience that if it is neglected, one risks emotional immaturity on a personal level, and social cataclysm on a community level.

The concept of Dr. Erickson is of importance in the further articulation of the Ethic of Reverence for the Dead because some individuals out of anxieties and fear of death create unnecessary and totally avoidable moral and emotional crisis overload by avoiding and denying the very rituals that have been developed over the centuries to help them deal wisely with the situations created by death. Sadly some individuals are very eloquent at articulating what they don't like about death rituals and ceremonies; but the same individuals rarely suggest anything better, wiser, or more insightful than the very rituals and activities that they have rejected. They are not creative because they have not thought this out ahead of time. All ethical inquiries start with human thought

This attitude goes quickly from ritual participation to ritual avoidance. It moves from something (even though it may well not be pleasurable) to nothing, and doing nothing when someone dies can be deadly to a grieving human being. In this instance ritual creativity freezes, and the Ethic of Reverence for the Dead once again collapses and valuable moral lessons about life stop.

At the heart of Dr. Erickson's thinking concerning rituals is the notion of personal moral maturity. For Dr. Erickson, balance between the opposite polarities of life is essential for maturation. Consider for a moment the example of the balance between the opposite ethical polarities of birth and death. The birth of a child is an event which simply leaves one filled with awe. Most often the birth of a child is an experience of joy. However, history has recorded clearly that for most of the history of the human race the birth of a child was far from a joyful experience. In fact it was an experience filled with anxieties and trepidations because of the simple fact that just 100 years ago parents did not expect their children to live. Infant mortality was highly a visible fact of life.

However today, and particularly in Western culture where we are blessed with highly sophisticated medical care and access even for the disenfranchised; the death of an infant is today grounds for a medical law suit. Babies are supposed to live – that is the expectation, but this is a terribly new, and terribly naïve expectation and it is a good example of the lopsided approach to life that rejects living in the tensions created by the polarities of life which Dr. Erickson is talking about.

For the first time in recorded history the meaningless idea that human beings can attain and live a carefree life is dangled in front of millions of innocent people who desperately believe that such a ridiculous notion about life is even possible. Think a moment of that idea: the carefree life. In such a fantasyland death and grief have little room, and once again the Ethic of Reverence for the Dead drops off people's mental screens, and moral maturity growth is once again stymied.

Dr. Eric Erickson
1902 - 1994

Dr. Erickson warns that for the moral development of personal maturity the human person must deal with both realities of life, the good and the bad, even if one is pleasant and the other unpleasant. In other words, the ethically mature person must live holistically between the tensions created by the opposite polarities of life.

To have authentic maturity, according to Dr. Erikson, the human needs to acknowledge the reality of death as much they easily acknowledge the reality of birth and life and participate in the human rituals which mark each of these rites of passage, the happy and the sad rites and rituals. Without this ethical balance and participation, Dr. Erickson says full maturation is impossible.

Dr. Rollo May (1909 – 1994) articulated this position when in his book "Existence" where he wrote these insightful words:

"The confrontation of death gives the most positive reality to life itself. It makes the individual existence real, absolute, and concrete. Death is the one fact of my life which is not relative, but absolute, and my awareness of this gives my existence

and what I do each hour an absolute quality taught."

In dealing realistically with death, it is within the context of the funeral ritual with the dead body image present that one sees the validation of the ethical, psychological and social values of preparing and preserving the dead and a reverential care of the dead come to full maturation. By the social structure of the funeral, the numinous of death is embraced and hence comprehended more completely. In a funeral there is a mature sense of ethical structure, a balance in ritual, a sense of security, and with the dead body image present, there is a sense of identity and reality. In the absence of the above ethical criterion the result is often isolation, insecurity, fantasy and unresolved grief which represent no balance at all and no ethics at all.

While the subject of death may never be fully comprehended we are able, by our ethical and social nature and mature sensitivities and the experience of the rites, rituals and ceremonies, to place the larger-than-life event of death into some type of manageable ethical form. Without this mature manageable form, Dr. Erickson's prediction of social and psychological cataclysm becomes reality. The inhuman death camps of Nazi Germany offer disturbing examples, in our own time, of the type of social, emotional, psychological and ethical deterioration which Dr. Erickson is referring.

In the death camps of Nazi Germany rites rituals and ceremonies were abandoned, the value of ethically caring for and having reverence for the dead was ignored with the result being personal catastrophe for millions upon millions and a legacy that the world is still ethically reeling more than 70 years later! Yet we still hear the thoughtless words, "When I'm dead just roll me over in a ditch."

At this juncture in our text an analysis of the value and benefits which are experienced within the specific ritual of the funeral needs to be given attention. We will explore and identify the essential components of funeral rituals as they are experienced within living the Ethic of Reverence for the Dead. To begin we will use Dr. William Lamer's definition of a funeral ritual, and then move into more specificity. Dr. Lamer's defines the funeral as: An organized, purposeful, time-limited, flexible, group centered response to the death of a single sacred decedent.

XIII. THE VALUE AND BENEFIT OF THE FUNERAL RITUALS BASED ON LIVING THE ETHIC OF REVERENCE FOR THE DEAD

From the ethical perspective of Reverence for The Dead let us be more analytical and specific and list these important human values and benefits one by one.

- Funeral rituals teach mutuality of recognition – in other words they teach a community to discriminate between good and bad. They afford us dramatic elaborations so we can remember this significant event in our life history. They also teach us the rules of the community in which we live. Mutuality of recognition simply means that people recognize what is happening.

- Funeral rituals are vital in dealing with the tensions of life, the polarities in life, and our opposites in life. Rituals help people find balance.

- Funeral rituals help integrate the creative possibilities in living life which are created by our opposites, i.e. the tension of life and death.

- Funeral rituals help break through idealized and exaggerated self-images and excessive individualization. When you are with others in funeral rituals you identify with others in the here and now.

- Funeral rituals state that we are interdependent co-beings. In interdependence with others I actually find independence because I belong somewhere and to some group.

- Funeral rituals interpret existence and challenges, the "take care of me first" attitudes. Funeral rituals challenge the excessive autonomy of self, and help people move from alienation, loneliness and fear, to assimilation, companionship and contact.

- Funeral rituals are a statement of social relationships existing in a community.

- Funeral rituals reflect the individual participant's ability to be interpersonal.

- Funeral rituals are repetitive, and as such function in giving a sense of security to the participants.

- Funeral rituals help individuals assimilate and cope with rapidly changing circumstances in life.

- Funeral rituals are instructional, interpretive and indoctrinating.

Obviously there is much going on here concerning the values and benefits of the funeral rituals for human beings.

The funeral ritual with the dead body present creates a morally truthful environment where recognition of a mature moral balance happens by enabling the bereaved to adapt to the reality of death by repeating the process of seeing the prepared and preserved body image. It also sets the foundations for the social psycho-drama that we call the death rituals, and these can take numerous forms and styles. To be effective the funeral rituals require the use of the perceptual dead body image of the deceased or relative symbols in order for the essential psychological detachments to occur.

In section XII of this text is listed the essential components of a funeral ritual that is based on a merging of Dr. Erickson's thinking with the conclusions made from this analysis, development and living the Ethic of Reverence for the Dead.

The funeral ritual values and benefits listed here are highly influenced by the presence or absence of people embracing the Ethic of Reverence for the Dead. Embracing the ethic affirms our recognizing the sacred decedent and the living as essential parts of each of the points just listed concerning the value and benefits of the funeral rituals.

In the absence of the ethic however, in the rejection consciously or unconsciously of this ethic which is behind and motivating all funeral rituals worldwide, the haunting question can be asked, "Have you actually thought this important subject out to its conclusion?" As anyone can readily see this subject requires thought, not a quick off the cuff answer. Thinking about the meaning of the Ethic of Reverence for the Dead, and what my answers to this meaning is for me personally does make all the difference in the world when the Grim Reaper makes his inevitable visit to us all.

XIV. THE PRACTICAL MODEL OF THE ETHIC OF REVERENCE FOR THE DEAD AS PRACTICED IN THE PREPARATION AND PRESERVATION OF THE DEAD

In order to accomplish all that has been discussed concerning articulating and daily maintaining the Ethic of Reverence for the Dead, one essential ingredient is desperately needed: TIME.

Consider the following points:

1. To wisely implement the ethical, psychological and sociological values of death rites rituals and ceremonies, people need time. We live in a throw-away society which does not value slowing down, but in the instance of death, this slowing-down process is vital and healthy. People need time to organize rites, rituals and ceremonies, to think, to participate, and to make decisions. In a very real sense each issue that we have considered in this text is of great importance to healthy mourning and requires time to simply think.

Time is required for the bereaved person to assimilate all that has happened, and the bereaved has the right to defend and demand that they be given their time.

2. Because of the depth of any issue relating to death, it is important that the bereaved person is offered the opportunity to incorporate into their lives the reality of the death situation. Concepts that is as ponderous as the reality of death and the Ethic of Reverence for the Dead must not be rushed.

3. The impact of the time issue is made all the more important, and the practical value of educated preparation and preservation is magnified all the more when one is made aware of and truly appreciates and understands the rapidity of decomposition. Preparation and preservation slows natural decomposition temporarily and hence affords the bereaved this all-important time that they need to make once-in-a-lifetime decisions and have the un-offensive dead body present at death rituals.

Preparation and preservation also serve a very practical use in that it renders the body inoffensive and makes it presentable. This is called the aesthetic value of preparation and preservation of the dead. The purpose of preparation and preservation in making the dead body presentable is NOT to create an illusion, but to create the remembered perceptual body image, a modern day effigy.

Preparation and preservation of the dead also serves as an emotional buffer when the living encounters a traumatic mode of death. The reality of traumatic death may be too burdensome a sight for the bereaved. The process of preparation and preservation and beautification aids in the restoration of the person and of their remembered body image tastefully with sensitivity and dignity. This is done not to mask reality, but to give the bereaved a body image that their perceptual pattern of recognition remembers and that is tactful and gently manageable.

The prepared and preserved dead body, which represents the remembered body image to the bereaved, affects and affords every valid opportunity for the survivors to be able to establish the reality of death. There exists no documentation of an inherent need for a bereaved person to be faced with the graphic raw details of a traumatic death visually. The reality of death is established by utilizing the restored remembered body image. The bereaved should know the truth of the circumstances of the death but not in an unkind and thoughtless manner. By using the time proven skills and talents and the values to humanity inherent in the preparation and preservation, beautification and restorative of the dead, this tough truth can be established in a more genteel and professional manner. This moral option to the bereaved is a core part of the Ethic of Reverence for the Dead.

Preparation and preservation also serves a very practical need because the American culture is very mobile – we move around all the time. The average American family moves once every four years. Many dead human remains are transported daily for dispositions "back home." It takes time to arrange the necessary burial and transportation for sanitation and health measures. Preparation and preservation procedures for the dead also offer the culture the time and assurance that the remembered body image will temporarily remain intact and recognizable while arrangements are made and transportation for the dead body is completed.

Finally, preparation and preservation practices today, as they have in the past, reflect the technology of the age. In ancient times, as we have seen, people used herbs and spices to maintain a type of odor control and primitive preservation. Today our basic intent is the same, but instead of herbs and spices we use sophisticated chemicals that have been developed by educated chemists. Early embalmers had to contend with lengthy and hazardous embalming procedures. Today the preparation and preservation process is efficient and sophisticated due to the advancements in mortuary technology.

In summary of the practical model, we can conclude that preparing and preserving a dead human body provides an efficient, simple and inexpensive manner of restoring and presenting the dead human body while enabling family and friends time to adjust to the loss, conduct ceremonies of remembrance, and ethically care for their dead. In a society and culture as developed, diverse, and mobile as any in the history of the world, preparation and preservation has been accepted as the most practical, economical and ethical manner of treatment of the dead.

This is a review of the major points of Part III this text:

1.   The Ethic of Reverence for the Dead addresses and articulates that death is a larger-than-life experience which is referred to as a numinous experience. The dead human body is the symbolic image of death which is rooted in the collective unconscious. In order to comprehend the larger-than-life experience of death, people must place the death experience into a ritualistic framework, with the body present as death's ultimate symbol. Rituals are the only human-made creation that can adequately deal with the numinous experience.

2.   The Ethic of Reverence for the Dead maintains at its core that having the prepared and preserved body image present at the funeral ritual allows the bereaved to place complex emotions of the numinous experience of death into a more simplified, structural form. The viewing of the dead body also aids in securing consistent human identification from one generation to another by repeating the time honored traditions of our ancestors' death rituals. This is an ethical and wise thing to do.

The dead body image of the deceased has been utilized for centuries to aid in identifying who we are as a family, community and even nation. Whether it is the Neanderthal, the ancient Egyptians or modern humankind, people relate to the reality of death by seeing the body image of the corpse. This is a universal need to the bereaved, for every bereaved person is working out of the same collective unconscious. The practice of contemporary preparation and preservation reflects an effective means of meeting the fundamental need of the bereaved to establish the reality of death with ethical sensitivities by implementing the technological knowledge and abilities that we have today; and because of the economical nature of preparation and preservation, every bereaved person can make use of its value and benefit.

3.   The Ethic of Reverence for the Dead maintains that the value of modern preparation and preservation is further validated by the essential place the sacred dead body plays in the inherent process of death rituals. We now know that the practice of contemporary preparation and preservation reflects ethical wisdom, healthy psychology, interpersonal sociology, and moral behaviors.

The art and science of preparation and preservation ultimately arrives at its essence by the ethical standard and practical moral utility it affords society. By living the Ethic of Reverence for the Dead we offer people time to make decisions, we afford an ongoing tradition to reverently care for the dead that is as ancient as civilization itself and we utilize all the wonders of modern technology in an economical manner. This is the moral thing to do.

XV. THE ESSENTIAL ETHICAL AND MORAL INVENTORY OF THE MEANING OF THE ETHIC OF REVERNCE FOR THE DEAD

- The ethic truthfully confronts the moral need to establish the reality of death.

- The ethic embraces the wisdom of the mature attitude towards death which is comprised of three moral actions:

  DEATH IS UNIVERSAL
  DEATH IS INEVITABLE
  DEATH IS IRREVERSABLE

- The ethic fully recognizes the validity of moral death teachings contained in history, theology, philosophy, psychology, sociology and religion.

- The ethic requires human moral action.

- The ethic was developed centuries ago in response to the human moral needs for help in times of death and grief.

- The ethic addresses practical moral concerns for the treatment of the dead.

- The ethic is the custodial responsibility of death care professionals who subscribe to the ethic and conduct their person in a consistent manner with the principles of the ethic.

- The ethic possesses at its core the idea of the moral cultural universal.

- The moral power and authority of the ethic is expressed most fully in rites, rituals and ceremonies.

- The moral power and authority of the ethic is expressed most fully in the preparation and preservation of the dead by the living.

- All memorials worldwide are tangible moral testimonies of the existence of the Ethic of Reverence for the Dead.

- The Ethic of Reverence for the Dead has at its core moral world religious thinking.

- The ethic has at its core human attachments and the human ability to reach for high moral standards.

- The Ethic of Reverence for the Dead should not be morally underestimated or unrecognized.

- The ethic needs moral attention and constant moral nurturing by the living.

- The ethic defends the human being's moral right to establish the reality of death.

- The ethic requires frequent thought, discussion and ongoing moral articulation.

- The ethic acknowledges truthfully the fact of physical death and its moral consequences to the living.

- The ethic acknowledges truthfully the fact of human grief and its moral consequences to the living.

- The ethic possesses the moral authority of truth.

- The ethic rejects the idea that human beings are mere biological events as immoral.

- The ethic rejects the idea as immoral that because you are dead means you are not human, and hence not of any value and purpose.

- The ethic holds at its core the inherent ancient moral values of death rites, rituals, and ceremonies which are for the living.

- The ethic embraces and fully recognizes the numinous experience.

- The Ethic of Reverence for the Dead is the foundational ethical position that morally validates the profession of funeral service.

- The ethic morally abhors the lack of ethical care of the dead in way, form or manner.

- The ethic is morally fragile and can easily be corrupted.

- The Ethic of Reverence for the Dead principles can be practiced by all human beings by implementing rites, rituals and ceremonies.

- The ethic consists of manifesting and exhibiting a consistent and progressive moral attitude, action and practice in showing respect and honor to all the dead in both thought and actions.

XVI. CONCLUSION

All professions, in order to lay serious claim to validity and worth in noble and ideal purposes, must ground their mission and careers with all sincerity and devotion in one supreme objective and absolute ethic.

In 1936 Dr. Albert Schweitzer (1875 – 1965), the world famous missionary physician, theologian, musician, philosopher and Nobel Peace Prize laureate published in the periodical **_Christendom_** his magnum opus article entitled "Reverence for Life." In this article Dr. Schweitzer said that anything that revered life is an ethical good, and anything that dishonored life was an ethical bad.

Dr. Schweitzer's famous Ethic of Reverence for Life, which Schweitzer himself claimed as his greatest legacy and contribution to humanity deserves a balancing opposite, and that balance is found within the ethical substance of the Ethic of Reverence for the Dead. For in the final analysis this dual concept of Reverence for Life anchored together indelibly with Reverence for the Dead opens the real possibility of the individual's greater sense of who they are by navigating a way towards the admirable human goal of enhancing and maturing both human nature and the human soul. It is good for humankind to revere the dead so that humankind can equally revere the living, for they morally go hand in hand and absolutely cannot be separated. In the end the Ethic of Reverence for the Dead is the Ethic of Reverence for Life.

For the moral and ethical authenticity of this great profession, we as funeral directors anchor as our claim to nobility and idealism and as the bedrock moral foundation in our ministries as both caretakers of the dead, and caregivers to the living to the Ethic of Reverence for the Dead.

DR. ALBERT SCHWEITZER
Physician, Philosopher, Theologian, Musician
1952 Recipient of the Nobel Peach Prize
1875 – 1965

XVII. GLOSSARY OF TERMS

- **MORALITY**: Morality puts the ethical theory into action or not. Morality refers to an individual's own principles regarding right or wrong, which may not be influenced by any ethical theory whatsoever. Morality has two subdivisions – subjective morality and objective morality.

  a) Subjective morality: this is the thought that morality is relative to one's own society only. Here morality is determined only by the individuals. Morality becomes a matter of taste. Another term for subjective morality is "Ethical Relativism". Modern people many times subscribe to this ethical approach.

  b) Objective morality: this approach to morality quests for the objective and absolute ethical standard and principle. This approach asks if there are norms or ethical standards or principles that apply to all. This is the approach most philosophers take. The Ethic of Reverence for the Dead is an objective, absolute moral standard and principle.

- **ETHICS**: Statements about human behavior in terms of good and bad. Ethics is a branch of philosophy that studies norms which govern individual conduct, and guides ones behaviors. This can be seen as a practical philosophy that guides as to what one ought and should do. Ethics also refers to the theory of thought behind the principles and standards. Many professions provide ethical principles and standards to their members. Ethics develops the theory.

- **CONUNDRUM**: This is a situation where there is no clear right answer or no good solution. Ethical conundrums create frustration and confusion. For this reason philosophers strive for absolute objective ethical standards and principles.

- **ETHICAL EVALUATIVE CRITERIA**: Five standards used in academia to evaluate moral subjects: human nature, moral feelings, consequences of the act, universal convictions, and religious thought as a guide.

- **PRIMAL EMOTIVE INSTINCTS**: Impulses or powerful motivations which are primal, of first or chief importance, which link us to our own ancient ancestors but which can be repressed.

- **NEANDERTHAL:**   Primitive, unenlightened, old-fashioned, reactionary.

    a) Neanderthal man: Member of an extinct subspecies of humans.   Homo sapiens neaderthalensis that inhabited Europe and West and Central Asia c. 100,000 – 40,000 B.C.

- **RALPH STEFAN SOLECKI: (1917 -)** Is an American Archaeologist. Born in New York City in 1917, he is a former member of the faculty at Columbia University. His best known excavations were at the Neanderthal site at Shanidar Cave in Iraq.

- **SHANIDAR CAVE – FLOWER BURIALS:** Is an archaeological site in the Zargros Mountains in Northern Iraq. Dr. Ralph Solecki yielded nine skeletons of Neanderthals of varying ages and states of preservations. One skeleton titled "Shanidar IV" provided evidence of Neanderthal burial rituals. The body was positioned so he was lying on his left side in a partial fetal position, and soil samples from around the body gathered for pollen analysis discovered whole clumps of flower pollen suggesting that entire flowering plants has been placed on top of the grave.

- **ARLETTE LEROI-GOURHAN: (1913 – 2005)** Famous French botanist who assisted Dr. Solecki in identifying the different flower pollen around the flower burials deep inside the Shanidar Cave.

- **THANATOPSIS:**   Written by American poet William Cullen Bryant when he was 17, the title is from the Greek *Thanatos* (death) and *opsis* (sight). *Thanatopsis* starts by talking about nature's ability to make us feel better. The voice of nature also tells us that when we die, we won't be alone. Every person who has ever lived is in the ground (Bryant calls this "the great tomb of man"). This idea was meant to be comforting and the lengthy poem ends by telling us to think of death like a happy, dream-filled sleep. This poem was the blockbuster in 1811 and made Bryant famous.

- **WILLIAM EWART GLADSTONE: (1809 – 1898)** Four time Prime Minister of Great Britain. Author of the famous ethical statement which begins: "Show me the manner in which a nation...."

- **BENJAMIN FRANKLIN: (1706 – 1705 O.S. – 1790):** Famous American sage, thinker, inventor and diplomat.

- **THE BOOK OF TOBIT:** A book contained in the "Apocrypha" which is considered non-canonical by certain religious organizations. This book tells the story of a righteous Israelite named Tobit. He is particularly noted for his diligence in attempting to provide proper burials for the fallen Israelites. The seventh corporal act of mercy *burial of the dead* has its roots in the Book of Tobit.

- **JESSICA MITFORD: (1917 – 1996)** Author, journalist, activist. Her most famous book was *The American Way of Dead* where she ridiculed the manner in which the dead are cared for in the United States.

- **CORPORAL WORKS OF MERCY:** The Works of Mercy or Acts of Mercy are actions and practices within Christianity in general that expects all believers to perform, and are a means of grace, which aid in sanctification. The Works of Mercy have been traditionally divided into two categories, with seven elements each: The Corporal Works of Mercy which concern the material needs of others, and the Spiritual Works of Mercy which concern the spiritual needs of others. The seventh Corporal Work of Mercy is **"To Bury the Dead."**

- **JOSEPH OF ARIMATHEA:** According to the Gospels he was the man who donated his own prepared tomb for the burial of Jesus. He is mentioned in all four Gospels. In the Gospel of Luke the account goes on to relate the great care that Joseph of Arimathea took wrapping Jesus' body in preparation for entombment. Joseph of Arimathea is the patron saint of funeral directors.

- **ATTACHMENT THEORY:** Describes the dynamics of long-term relationships between humans. Its most important tenet is that an infant needs to develop a relationship with at least one primary caregiver for social and emotional development to occur normally. The body image of the deceased is related to human attachments. Even when no clear attachments are present the morality of the Ethic of Reverence for the Dead still requires moral action on the part of the living.

- **SEPARATION THEORY:** Describes the dynamic of when

attachments end and severed, caused by death separation or human communication and interaction separation.

- **DEATH ILLITERACY:** Contemporary condition whereby the personal awareness of death has not been cognitively developed in a human being. It is similar to reading illiteracy where no one has taught a person about the skills necessary to read.

- **SHIVA:** Hebrew word literally meaning "seven" is the week-long mourning period in Judaism for first-degree relatives: father, mother, daughter, brother, sister and spouse. The ritual is referred to as "sitting Shiva." Immediately after burial people assume the status of mourner. This state lasts for seven days during which family members traditionally gather in one home and receive visitors. At the funeral mourners traditionally rend (tear) an outer garment in a ritual known as *keriah*. This garment is worn throughout Shiva.

- **SHOLOSHIM:** Hebrew word meaning "30". It is a 30-day mourning period in Judaism which includes Shiva. During this mourning period a man may not get married or attend a *mitzvah* (religious festival meal). Also men do not shave or get haircuts during this important mourning period.

- **FUNERAL EFFIGY:** Images of deceased royalty made out of wax or wood which were used to remind living people of what these important people looked like. Today modern preservation of a deceased accomplishes the same purpose but for a fraction of the cost. Effigy making is a lost art form.

- **DR. ERICH LINDEMANN:** (1900 – 2005) Harvard professor of psychiatry. Wrote the first academic paper documenting human grief *"The Symptomatology and Management of Acute Grief"* as a result of his study of the survivors of the Cocoanut Grove Fire in Boston in 1942. The Lindemann Psychiatric Center of Harvard Medical School is named in his honor.

- **REV. DR. EDGAR N. JACKSON:** (1910 – 1994) Pioneer author in the study of human grief. Dr. Jackson was a longtime professor of psychology at the New England Institute of Funeral Arts and Sciences in Boston as well as Boston University. He was the author of *Understanding Grief, the Many Faces of Grief, the Christian Funeral, How to Tell A Child about Death.*

- **GEOFFREY GORER:** (1905 – 1985) British anthropologist and author who made impressive contributions to the ethical care of the dead in world history and cultural anthropology.

- **DR. CARL G. JUNG:** (1875 – 1961) Founder of Analytical Psychology. A student of Dr. Freud in his early years, Dr. Jung was highly influential in both psychiatry and the study of religion.

- **DR. ERIC ERICKSON:** (1902 – 1994) He was a developmental psychologist and psychoanalyst who never earned a Bachelor's degree but taught at both Harvard and Yale. He is today known for his compelling theories of the psycho-social development of human beings. He coined the phrase "identity crisis."

- **RUDOLPH OTTO:** (1869 – 1937) Eminent German Lutheran theologian and scholar of comparative religions. His most famous work is *The Idea of the Holy* which was written in 1917. The book has never been out of print.

- **AUGUSTE COMPTE** (1779 – 1851) French philosopher. Compte was the founder of the academic discipline called *sociology.*

- **DR. SIGMUND FREUD** (1856 – 1939) Austrian neurologist known as one of the founding fathers of psychoanalysis.

- **COLLECTIVE UNCONSIOUS:** A term in analytical psychology coined by Dr. Carl G. Jung. Jung himself defined it this way: "My thesis then is as follows: in addition to our immediate consciousness, which is of a thoroughly personal nature and which we believe to be the only empirical psyche (even if we tack on the personal unconscious as an appendix), there does exists a second psychic system of a collective, universal, and impersonal nature which is identical in all human beings. This collective unconscious does not develop individually but is inherited. It consists of pre-existent forms, the **archetypes**, which can only become conscious secondarily and which gives definite form to certain psychic contents.

- **ARCHETYPE:** In Jungian psychology the archetypes refer to a collectively inherited unconscious idea, pattern of thought, image,

87

etc., universally present in individual psyches. Archetype can refer to a constantly recurring symbol or motif in literature, painting, religions, or mythology. This usage of the term draws from both comparative anthropology and Jungian archetypal theory. The dead human body is an archetypal image universal to every person on the earth.

- **SYMBOLS:** Symbols include archetypes, acts, artwork, events or natural phenomena. With this approach to symbols what a person is looking at has behind it a deeper meaning about life, death and the ultimate meaning of life. In Christianity the cross might be described as two pieces of wood attached at an angle – but if a person looks at this Christian symbol as to what invisibly is behind the symbol, limitless lessons about the meaning of life and death abound and flourish. Symbols are most effective when they appeal to both the intellect and emotions. **A symbol is a thing which is beside the thing that we see that leads to knowledge other than itself. This deeper notion of symbols helps people make an unknown reality known.** The prepared/preserved dead human body is the ultimate symbol of the reality of death and this symbol is a universal numinous.

- **"THE IDEA OF THE HOLY"** Rudolph Otto's seminal book where he sets for his concept of the numinous and numinous experiences in life. Viewing a dead human body qualifies as a numinous experience.

- **THE NUMINOUS:** This describes an experience that has the power to invoke fear and trembling, yet creates fascination and attraction; awe, wonder, highly attracted; transcendent, suggesting the presence of divinity – the powerful, personal feeling of being overwhelmed and inspired; the feeling that you are in the presence of God or something greater than yourself. Another phrase to describe the **larger-than-life** experience.

- **ONTOGENY OF RITUALIZATION:** An original term coined by Dr. Eric Erickson to describe the maturation processes in how a human being learns about the dynamics, meaning and use of rites, rituals and ceremonies in living a good healthy psychological and spiritual life. Dr. Erickson maintained that the individual or society could not survive without rites, rituals and ceremonies.

- **DR. ROLLO MAY:** **(1909 – 1994)** American Existential Psychologist who stressed living within the crises of life, and by recognizing the wisdom of rites, rituals and ceremonies as wise and careful coping mechanisms to help guide people through the crisis. Dr. May wrote: *Love and Will, Existences, and the Art of Counseling.*

- **ETHICAL EVALUATIVE CRITERIA:** The component subjects which are used in analyzing and articulating the principles and standards for a particular ethical topic. The criteria are:

  a) Human Nature.
  b) Consequences of the Act.
  c) Universal Convictions.
  d) Moral Feelings.
  e) Religious Convictions as a Guide.

- **REVERENCE:** A feeling or attitude of profound respect, usually reserved for the sacred or divine which is shown about in outward manifestation by a bow of the head, meditation, kneeing at prayer, introspection. The feelings of something being hallowed or exalted or to be in awe.

- **PREPARATION OF THE DEAD:** This right of the dead and the moral duty of the living to expect and maintain minimal standards of moral action that the sacred dead human being will remain in a state of honor, reverence and protection from the point and place of death to the point and place of final commitment of the sacred decedent. It is a fact that the sacred dead cannot take care of their bodies or defend their human dignity and because of this reality minimal attentive preparation and protection of the sacred dead body is part of the definition of the Ethic of Reverence for the Dead. This includes but is not limited to the following minimal measures of human moral attention and action:

  a) The sacred decedent is covered entirely at all times.
  b) No profanity is used around and in the presence of the sacred decedent.
  c) The environment where the sacred decedent is reposing will be clean, reverential, quiet and presentable at all times.
  d) To insure measures to safeguard the sacred decedent from harm.

- **PRESERVATION:** This is the expanded preparation by

preservation of the sacred dead human body by means of sophisticated chemicals accomplished though the work of graduate licensed professionals. Preservation makes it possible to have the sacred dead human body available and present in a non-offensive condition for important death rites, rituals and ceremonies. It is also a modern day effigy. It also gives the living time to make important once-in-lifetime decisions, such as travel and shipment of the decedent.

- **WILLIAM JAMES: (1842 – 1910)** Harvard psychologist. Wrote the 1902 classic, *The Varieties of Religious Experience.*

- **THE FUNERAL:** The funeral rite, rituals or ceremonies is an organized, purposeful, time limited, flexible, group centered response to dead. Please refer to section XIV of the text for the expanded list of the value and benefits experienced in observing funeral rituals.

- **DR. ALBERT SCHWEITZER: (1875 – 1965)** Developed the ethic of Reverence for Life. Dr. Schweitzer held Doctorate degrees in Music, Philosophy, Theology and Medicine. He won the 1952 Nobel Peace Prize for his lifelong work in being of service to others.

"Treat the living as though they are dying and treat the dead as though they are alive."

NIKOLAI BERDYAEV
1874 – 1948
Russian Christian
Existentialist Philosopher

ABOUT THE AUTHOR

Todd W. Van Beck has been serving the funeral profession for fifty years. He started his career at the Heafey & Heafey Mortuary in Omaha, Nebraska and throughout his career has been involved with every aspect of the purpose, meaning and benefit of funeral rituals and ceremonies, as well as the subjects of death, grief, bereavement care, funeral service history, as well as management issues in funeral service. Mr. Van Beck is an author, teacher, lecturer on an international basis. He has published over 600 professional articles as well as having written over 60 training programs. His book "Winning Ways" was published in 1998, and most recently he has published two new books, "Reverence for the Dead" and "The Story of Cremation." He was honored by the ICCFA Educational Foundation with their first "Landmark Career" award in 2014. Mr. Van Beck also holds an honorary doctorate degree from the Commonwealth Institute of Funeral Service. He is currently on the staff of the John A. Gupton College, in Nashville, Tennessee. He is married to Georgia who is a Clinical Supervisor with Hospice.

Made in the USA
Columbia, SC
06 September 2024

41930929R00054